Praise for *Collective Visioning*

"This inspiring and practical guide to community organizing should be read by everyone involved in the struggle for justice, democracy, and equal rights. Linda Stout knows how to bring people together to be agents of change. Read this book and find out how you can do this too."

—**John Shattuck, President and Rector, Central European University, and former US Assistant Secretary of State for Democracy, Human Rights, and Labor**

"Linda Stout's book represents decades of profound experience activating ordinary people to do extraordinary things! She inspires people to take action toward the kinds of future they truly want, to experiment with expanding their sense of empowerment, build a cohort group for support, and get on with changing their world. Stout knows we proceed from 'the dream' outward into activism. She is a true master of inspire, inform, and activate. *Collective Visioning* is where it all begins."

—**Christina Baldwin, coauthor of *The Circle Way* and author of *Storycatcher***

"The peace movement is too intellectual. There needs to be a book that speaks to regular people. Linda has taken the research we did and made it real and accessible."

—**Elise Boulding, cofounder, International Peace Research Association, and author of *Cultures of Peace***

"Linda's book is urgently needed now. Many congregations are starting to engage in Appreciative Inquiry and visioning processes to identify hopes and dreams but lack the tools that can translate these into concrete action."

—**Susan Leslie, Director, Office for Congregational Advocacy and Witness, Unitarian Universalist Association of Congregations**

"Now more than ever our world needs to make use of Linda's heartfelt and innovative approaches to engage people of all backgrounds—including those whose voices are not often heard—in creating futures that work for all. Buy this accessible, straightforward guide today and make a difference tomorrow."

—**Amanda Trosten-Bloom, Managing Director, Corporation for Positive Change, and coauthor of *The Power of Appreciative Inquiry***

"Linda's soul is well endowed with a generous, optimistic, and creative sense of the capacity for enlightenment and change for each fellow mortal, no matter what social class or ethnicity each represents. She offers opportunities for our democratic process to work, indeed, flourish, giving us hope in a climate so laden with negativity. Her book is most timely when we hunger for new approaches to solving so many problems eroding our communities."
—Loring Conant, Jr., MD, Assistant Professor of Medicine, Harvard Medical School

"Linda Stout is in a unique position for defining an inspiring new vision of community-based social change. For many years, she has brought a healing, collaborative, sensitive approach to working with groups and social movements. She deeply understands their hopes as well as their challenges and fully appreciates the wide range of diversity across many aspects of our society. I know of no other activist, leader, or visionary who possesses such an all-encompassing and perceptive understanding. To listen to Linda is to be inspired, to gain new hope that a fundamental transformation of our culture is not only possible but may be much nearer than we expect. A book that carries her vision around the country to new audiences is a valuable contribution."
—Dr. Ron Miller, President, New Visions Foundation

"This book does not focus on all that is wrong with the world but holds fast to the centrality of vision, hope, and persistence for real change. Linda Stout's life embodies the courage to tackle hard issues, such as race, class, gender, and sexual orientation, from a perspective of inclusiveness and justice for all. This book is the next logical extension of her readiness to speak truth and encourages us that real love is about caring for all people, not just the ones who look and sound like us."
—Rev. John H. Vaughn, Director, Twenty-First Century Foundation

Collective Visioning

Collective
Visioning

HOW GROUPS CAN WORK TOGETHER
FOR A JUST AND
SUSTAINABLE FUTURE

Linda Stout

Berrett–Koehler Publishers, Inc.
San Francisco
a BK Currents book

361·8

Berrett-Koehler Publishers, Inc.
235 Montgomery Street, Suite 650
San Francisco, CA 94104-2916
Tel: (415) 288-0260   Fax: (415) 362-2512   www.bkconnection.com

Ordering Information

Quantity sales. Special discounts are available on quantity purchases by corporations, associations, and others. For details, contact the "Special Sales Department" at the Berrett-Koehler address above.

Individual sales. Berrett-Koehler publications are available through most bookstores. They can also be ordered directly from Berrett-Koehler: Tel: (800) 929-2929; Fax: (802) 864-7626; www.bkconnection.com

Orders for college textbook/course adoption use. Please contact Berrett-Koehler: Tel: (800) 929-2929; Fax: (802) 864-7626.

Orders by U.S. trade bookstores and wholesalers. Please contact Ingram Publisher Services, Tel: (800) 509-4887; Fax: (800) 838-1149; E-mail: customer.service@ingram-publisherservices.com; or visit www.ingrampublisherservices.com/Ordering for details about electronic ordering.

Berrett-Koehler and the BK logo are registered trademarks of Berrett-Koehler Publishers, Inc.

Printed in the United States of America

Berrett-Koehler books are printed on long-lasting acid-free paper. When it is available, we choose paper that has been manufactured by environmentally responsible processes. These may include using trees grown in sustainable forests, incorporating recycled paper, minimizing chlorine in bleaching, or recycling the energy produced at the paper mill.

Library of Congress Cataloging-in-Publication Data

Stout, Linda.
  Collective visioning : how groups can work together for a just and sustainable future / Linda Stout.
      p. cm.—(BK currents)
  Includes bibliographical references and index.
  ISBN 978-1-60509-882-1
  1. Community development. 2. Sustainable development. 3. Social justice. 4. Self-actualization (Psychology) 5. Group decision making. I. Title.
  HN49.C6S764 2011
  307.3'4091724—dc22   2011007844

FIRST EDITION
15 14 13 12 11   9 8 7 6 5 4 3 2 1

Cover design: Barbara Haines
Cover art:@iStockphoto.com/Mikosch
Design and composition: Beverly Butterfield, Girl of the West Productions
Copyediting: PeopleSpeak
Indexing: Rachel Rice

I write this book in honor of my parents, Kathleen and Herschel Stout, who modeled core values of honesty, respect, and compassion while teaching me principles of equality, justice, and peace. But most of all, my parents supported me and believed that I could accomplish anything I wanted to. I deeply miss them and know they are proud of who I am today.

contents

preface

I HAVE come from growing up in extreme poverty to being a leader of a national organization. If anyone had told me when I began working—first, in tobacco, later in a hosiery mill, and then moving my way up to be a secretary— that I could make real change in the world and actually write books, I would have looked at that person as if he or she were talking another language. I was not the leader type and did not have the education or confidence to do any of these things.

When I first started organizing, I went to trainings that were pretty conventional. They taught me a lot about working for change. I also began to ask why some of the techniques I was learning didn't work for me and other poor people in my own community. I would go to leadership workshops and leave feeling that I could never be a leader, or I'd go to fund-raising workshops and leave knowing that I could never raise money. And I always knew I could not write!

Obviously, that has changed. It took a long time for me to find my own voice and power, but I did, and I've helped others find theirs, too. Still, over the years, I've battled a self-doubting voice that says, "I'm not good enough to be

xii   COLLECTIVE VISIONING

a leader or to write a book." The messages I got as a young person who grew up poor and the assumptions that some people made about me because I did not get to graduate from college have stayed with me. Even though I've been exploring what it means to be a leader for decades, and even though this is my second book, the voices of doubt are still there. My experiences have shaped how I think and work now. My passion and my life have come to be about making this world a place where all people can feel powerful and take leadership in creating a just and sustainable world.

I started organizing for peace when I lived in Charleston, South Carolina, and helped start a Quaker meeting there. I had no clue how to organize around peace, but I met another young woman named Carol who came to the meeting because she was also interested in starting a peace group. She was about my age but very different. While I was working as a secretary, she was a hippie with tattered Birkenstocks held together by duct tape who lived on an old sailboat. We went to my house after the Quaker meeting and made a plan for the first meeting of our own group. I had been looking for someone who could lead a peace group that I could be a part of. As we started to put together the agenda, she said, "You have to be the leader."

I looked at her in shock and said, "I can't do that."

She said, "You have to. Look at me. No one would listen to me!"

I knew she was right. People would discount her not only because of how she looked and dressed but because she wasn't southern. I was scared, but all it took was that one person to help create a plan and to support me. We began to organize. Very soon, a number of interns and medical students joined our group. They had been motivated by a film from Physicians for Social Responsibility about nuclear winter, an environmental catastrophe many believed would happen if a nuclear war took place, making the earth uninhabitable for most life.

We soon joined up with the Nuclear Weapons Freeze Campaign, a national effort to stop and disarm nuclear weapons. The campaign grew powerfully and successfully, and eventually, I was asked to serve on the board. After Ronald Reagan's election as president of the United States, the Nuclear Weapons Freeze Campaign, the Committee for a Sane Nuclear Policy, and Physicians for Social Responsibility mushroomed into mass movements. Historian Lawrence Wittner refers to this history in his article "What Activists Can Learn from the Nuclear Freeze Moment." In June 1982, nearly a million Americans turned out for a rally in New York City against the nuclear arms race, the largest political demonstration up to that point in US history. The nuclear freeze campaign drew the backing of major religious bodies, professional organizations, and labor unions. Supported by 70 percent or more of the population, the freeze was endorsed by 275 city governments, 12 state legislatures, and the voters in nine out of ten states where it was placed on the ballot in the fall of 1982.[1]

Thanks to popular pressure, the administration largely lost the battle to develop its favorite nuclear weapon, the MX missile, securing funding for only 50 of the 200 originally proposed. The administration also opened negotiations on eliminating strategic nuclear weapons, abandoned plans to deploy the neutron bomb in Western Europe, and accepted the limits of the unratified SALT (Strategic Arms

Limitation Talks) II treaty (though previously Reaganites had lambasted the treaty as a betrayal of US national security). Moreover, according to Wittner, the president began to proclaim that "a nuclear war cannot be won and must never be fought."[2]

Historian Lawrence Wittner concludes, "If this dramatic reversal in US public policy could be produced when the Reaganites controlled Washington politics, then a similar turnabout can be fostered today."[3]

Despite the huge successes, the movement has dwindled in numbers and lost the power it once had. There was a brief rise at the beginning of the first Gulf War (1990–91) and again at the beginning of the second Iraq War (2003 to present), but soon those gains fell away as well. Many people and organizations are still devoting themselves and their resources to peace, but nothing currently compares to the earlier powerful numbers of the freeze movement.

So why did such a powerful movement fall apart? Why is it almost nonexistent in most people's minds and in the news today? I believe that there are three major reasons.

First, the national peace movement failed to mobilize most working-class people, low-income people, and people of color. Certainly, the members of this movement made valiant efforts, but they were unsuccessful because of their lack of attention to cultural differences and education levels and their inability to make the connections to the economic issues facing poor people.

Second, many of us in this powerful movement shared a sense of doomsday and worked mostly from a place of anger and fear. We didn't understand how to move that anger and fear into sustainable, positive action. We used films and maps to show what would happen in the event of a nuclear bomb explosion and how the radioactive fallout and the environmental effects of a nuclear winter would destroy the earth as we know it. We demonstrated the firepower of nuclear weapons in the world with BBs. We would ask people to close their eyes and imagine that the next sound they heard was equivalent to the total firepower contained in all the weapons used in World War II. We would then drop a single BB into a metal can. Again, we would ask them to think of all the firepower used in World War II, such as bullets, bombs, grenades, and the nuclear bombs dropped on Japan. And again, we would drop a single BB. We would explain that since World War II, nuclear weapons had multiplied significantly, primarily owned by the United States and Russia. Then we would ask them to close their eyes and tell them the next sound they would hear was equivalent to the nuclear weapons present now; it did not include bombs, grenades, bullets, or other conventional weapons. We would slowly pour 2,225 BBs into the can.[4] I remember doing this exercise many times and seeing a look of fear and horror and sometimes tears on people's faces. Many people joined the campaign out of their horror and fear of a nuclear war.

Third, and I believe most important, the freeze movement fell apart because it was *a movement without a vision* of what a peaceful and cooperative world would look like. I still deeply care about this issue, but when I was in the middle of the campaign built on fear, I suffered from nightmares and constant fear that life as I knew it would be destroyed at any moment. Many others I have talked to who were part of the beginning of this movement say the same thing. Others compare it to the fear of environmental and climate disaster today. I believe it is impossible to sustain a long-term movement without a positive vision of what we can accomplish, what the world would look like on the other side.

So, instead of continuing to focus on the doomsday pictures, I now ask, "What do we want the world to look like?" Those who work for change from a place of joyfulness and hope are more able to be effective, reach more people, and win what they want. The movement is more sustainable.

I have been accused by other activists of being utopian or too optimistic, of not looking at reality. That is far from my truth. A vision in itself is a critique of the present times. Sometimes people think of collective visioning as an escape mechanism or as not being grounded in reality, but how can we move toward what we want if we can't envision what it looks like? That doesn't mean we don't acknowledge the current realities we are up against, but it's a different frame to work from—a frame I believe can sustain us and give us hope against the horrifying issues and problems facing us today.

People are already afraid. But I know that if people had a vision filled with hope of what could be, knew what they needed to act on, and believed in their power to make it happen, we could create a just and peaceful world today. This book is my next step in helping us get there.

LINDA STOUT
Belchertown, MA
March 2011

Creating a
Different Future

This book is for all of us looking for a different, more fulfilling, and sustainable way to work that creates real and lasting change for ourselves and future generations.

In *Collective Visioning*, you will learn how to create a vision with others of the world you want to live in and how to work together to make it happen. This is a guide to how to change your community, your organization, your faith group, your school, and beyond. I know collective visioning works for many different kinds of people and organizations because I've used it with so many different groups: small gatherings of junior high school students in New Orleans after Katrina, urban immigrant communities, activists in Iowa, hundreds of churches and spiritual gatherings, students at Ivy League universities, networks of educators, and folks working (with stunning success) to get out the vote in North Carolina, among many others.

In my work for justice over the past thirty years, I have seen many amazing accomplishments. In the chapters to come I will tell you the stories of how some of them happened. At the same time, I know that many things have continued to get worse for many people and that there is greater poverty, homelessness, and economic and environmental crises than we've seen in many decades. Yet I hold enormous hope about creating a future that works for us all.

Understanding the value and power of collective visioning for the future of our communities and our world is critical to our ability to inspire others to move to action. Many of us who have worked for change have been focused on problems and creating strategies and plans to address these problems. By always focusing on the problems, we get locked into patterns of negativity and critique, not allowing ourselves the ability to look at the bigger picture or set goals that inspire and help us and others through the hard work of change. Our focus is on what we are against rather than what we are for. People who join in the struggle for change often come from a place of anger and fear. This makes emotional sense given the urgency of current problems, but it isn't sustainable for the long haul.

Authors Paul Ray and Sherry Anderson point out in their book, *The Cultural Creatives: How 50 Million People Are Changing the World,* that the majority of people in this country hold positive values: a concern about the environment, peace, homelessness, hunger, and poverty. At the same time, their research found that a lot of these people are turned off by movements on both the right and the left, which they see as extremist, negative, and judgmental.

As a result of these perceptions, many people who care about the environment and social justice stay away from organizations in favor of individual actions such as volunteering, carrying a cloth bag to the grocery store, recycling, donating food, or working for a food bank on holidays. While all of these actions are important and worthy, we need efforts that inspire people to address the larger root problems we face.

When people vision together, they get excited and become much more invested in creating the future of their dreams. They begin to take more ownership in their organization, school, or community and take on responsibility for the plan they create together. They begin to say "we" and "our" and feel that they are a critical part of the process. They volunteer to do more and are more accountable than is usually seen in groups that are not grounded in a collective vision and action plan. People develop a deep sense of community and connection. The work comes from a place of joy and hope.

In Spirit in Action, my current organization, we have experienced this many times in the work of building networks. It's amazing to see how many people step forward to help when times get tough. They also help each other, sharing resources and skills. These are much more connected and deeper networks than most. Those in a group share a sense of being part of a community, a family, even though people in most of our networks are scattered across the country.

When we ground our work in a collective positive vision, the process builds a strong and connected community. Not only are we more successful in winning the issues, we transform ourselves, our communities, and beyond. We look at what we need to do in a more cooperative, resourceful, and inclusive way than when we are focused on just fixing problems. While we take into consideration urgent and current issues, our ongoing action, based on a collective vision, is strategic and intentional. Not only does visioning guide our work, it inspires and motivates people to stay in it for the long haul despite the hardships. It leads us toward lasting, proactive, positive action for change.

We need to work together to come up with a collective vision for what is possible, identify seeds of hope already planted, and then learn how to make real and lasting change. We need to acknowledge and heal from our fears—the fear of others, of global warming, of terrorist attacks, and of losing our identities—and learn how to transform these fears into real action for change.

Most of us will need to relearn what it means to live in a community, that is, a diverse community that goes beyond our usual circle of friends or those who think just like us. If we understand what we can gain from being part of deep, connected, and diverse communities, we can learn how to work in a way that is joyful, fulfilling, and life sustaining.

I've witnessed this kind of work, and sometimes I've been part of making it happen. I want to make it easier for you to be part of it, too. When people vision collectively, their achievements are amazing. For example,

• In North Minneapolis, people have a vision of reclaiming and rebuilding their neighborhood from a place of violence and decay into a place of community involvement, beauty, and safety. Their vision is to have all children born in the community be prepared for college when they graduate from high school. Not only are people from the community committed to this goal, but also elected officials (including the mayor), artists, businesspeople, and many others are working together to make this vision a reality. They have already bought many foreclosed homes and rebuilt them as sustainable green homes and have rebuilt businesses owned and controlled by community people. They have also created a youth art center, an arts park, a youth-run bakery, and a community theater with youth involvement and training.

- A poor community in Tallulah, Louisiana, fought for over ten years to close down one of the most abusive, oppressive prisons in the country—a prison that incarcerated young people. After community members won this important fight, the state immediately voted to reopen the prison as an adult penitentiary. Not until the community members turned to visioning—"What do we want instead of a prison?"—were they successful in getting the state to vote to close down the prison with the idea of turning it into a community college.

- Children in New Orleans changed the way new schools are being rebuilt after Hurricane Katrina to include community gardens, green space for outdoor classes, restorative justice circles, and cafeterias that serve healthy food and have hand-washing stations.

I will tell you more about how collective visioning worked in New Orleans and Tallulah later in the book.

Imagine if these examples were all seeds. What could happen if our whole country worked together collectively to grow these seeds into nationwide and worldwide actions?

Imagine if we could mobilize to elect leaders dedicated to *real* democracy, leaders who truly represent us and what we care about and are accountable to us, the people, rather than corporate power and money.

I started Spirit in Action in January 2000 after an extensive listening project with activists from all over the country conducted in 1998–99 by Peace Development Fund while I was the executive director there. We asked people who worked on many different issues at every level what was needed to build a powerful movement to create a just and equitable world. When we started Spirit in Action, we continued this exploration and began to identify clear issues that needed to be addressed.

We decided to search for answers about three powerful issues people had identified. The first issue was that we activists were really good at talking about what we were against but not good at talking about what we wanted to build—the kind of world we wanted to live in. We lacked a collective vision that we could all rally around and work together to create.

The second issue was all the ways that people get divided—by race, class, age, gender, sexual preference, and religious or spiritual beliefs, as well as by competition for turf, credit, and funding. People felt that we needed a new way to learn to work together and that the ways we were doing antiracism and anticlassism work needed to be more inclusive. We needed to work to heal divisions rather than polarize people.

The third issue was what I identify as "spirit" or "heart." I use the word "spirit" in the broadest sense. People talked about what motivated them to work for justice. Many were motivated by religious and spiritual beliefs. Others were moved by parents or other people they'd known who had deeply influenced them. Some had experienced or seen injustice in their lifetimes and, as a result, felt called to work for a different kind of world. All of them came into this work from deeply held heart or spirit values, but often they felt isolated because they were unable to express those values. People felt uncomfortable about sharing their whole selves in diverse groups. Many also felt that we often didn't have time to work in a way that allowed us to bring our whole selves into the work. As a result, many felt disillusioned and angry and often spoke of burnout.

Many people we talked to felt that there had to be another way to work—a way that was inspiring and fulfilling. Spirit in Action was formed to begin to find answers about those three issues from other organizations and many individuals. Some of the answers we found are in this book.

My own spiritual practice came to be about listening. As a lifelong Quaker, listening to spirit led me to listen to what people needed, to what people weren't saying, and to the people who had no voice in the groups I was a part of. Eventually, I was listening to as many people as I could, including my friends and family of different political backgrounds—from extremist left to extremist right, and the many in between—to friends who were Buddhist, Quaker, atheist, Pagan, Fundamentalist Christian, Conservative Christian, Progressive Christian, Mormon, Jewish, Muslim, and agnostic. I even listened to people who had been members of the Ku Klux Klan. I realized that, deep down, most of us share many of the same fears and values. We all hope for a better future for our children and generations to come.

It is no secret that I am a spiritual person and very progressive in my political views. All of my friends know this, and I often have loving conversations with my conservative friends about our different beliefs. We learn from each other in powerful ways. My uncle Ed once started a conversation with "Well, I know you believe differently than I do, but I still love you, and I want you to read and think about this article about the war."

I said, "I love you, and I will read or think about this, but I would like for you to read and think about something I send to you." We agreed to do that.

My aunt Carolyn and uncle Ed talked with me about this book when I was first thinking about it. After we talked, they sent me several Bible verses about the importance of visioning, like this one, Proverbs 29:18: "Where there is no vision, the people perish."

So why am I writing this book about collective visioning at this time? Because I've seen people join together to make incredible changes in their communities and lives. I know that if we work together we can create a different world, not only in our lifetimes but for generations to come.

In this book I want to

- Tell stories of goals that have already been accomplished
- Give you guidelines on how to vision a collective future in order to create a just and sustainable world
- Help you learn how to start building deep and collaborative connections with others to work together for your visions
- Offer guidelines about how to build a stronger and more diverse community
- Empower you to work from a place of inspiration and joy

During the 2008 Obama campaign, I saw thousands of people, especially young folks, working for change because they had hope for the message of a different future. The message of hope and change energized and moved thousands of people to take action, many for the first time in their lives.

While it would be wonderful to think that electing the "right" president or other government official would solve all our problems, unfortunately we have a political system that is so driven by big money and corporate power that even people we have elected who share our values of justice and equity and want to make change often come up short of what they promise. It's easy for us to sit back and blame or resent the government, but the truth is, until a majority of people believe they have the power to create that kind of change, we will continue in the same way, with corporate power and money driving the policies that affect our lives.

We are now living in a time of great change and upheaval in our society. We see a level of decay of infrastructure, schools, jobs, government, and community we have not seen in decades. We have become a nation of individualists, reduced to protecting and building for ourselves, rather than for the good of the whole. We instinctively know how to be in community and to support each other—we saw examples of this after the September 11th bombing of the World Trade Center in New York and after Hurricane Katrina. At the same time, we saw examples of our divisions and fear of others in these catastrophes, divisions that oppressed people because of their race, ethnicity, class, and religion. The challenge is to figure out how we can build a sustainable culture of working together in a way that embraces all of the diversity that is our ultimate strength.

Many people feel helpless about making change in their lifetimes. The truth is that we all have the ability to make these changes, but only if we learn to understand the "other" and to act on what we really want for ourselves, our families, and the earth. In order to create a different future, we must first create a collective vision and learn to work together effectively to make it happen.

The popularity of self-help "visioning" books reflects a population hungry for hope and positive vision. However, the concepts in many of these books inspire people to create a vision for what they want personally. This moves them to an even more isolated, individualistic, and materialistic place and the belief that if you are not becoming wealthy or getting the perfect job, it's your fault for not thinking positively enough. There is a place for individual visions in my work, and I've included a chapter about them in this book, but when you begin to join your vision with those of others, true excitement and change begin to happen. I believe that this alternative message is what people are eager for—one that breaks our isolation, builds community, and most importantly, gives us hope for the future.

In this book, you will find that I often use the words "we" or "us" instead of "I" or "me." That is because so many people contributed to the formation of these ideas. Many of the ideas come from knowledge that has been with us for ages. Much of my methodology comes from Spirit in Action's first experimental Circles of Change. These took place all over the country, with twenty-seven trained facilitators. Hundreds of people who participated shared their knowledge and insights with us. Our methodology also came from many organizations that had information, insights, and strategies that we learned from. I list many of those in the resources at the end of the book. We also have a strong team of staff, volunteers, and consultants who have come together to help create the work we do today.

When I first started using visioning for myself and in my own community, I was not aware of the decades of research by sociologists, historians, futurists, and others about visioning. If you, like me, think you might find having a historical perspective and information on academic research about visioning useful to help you understand more deeply the role it can play in social change, you can find more about this work on my website.

In addition to our own collective knowledge, it's important to remember that we stand on the knowledge of many others who have passed their wisdom down to us. I have read about visioning in indigenous cultures that predate Christianity. I have learned from my elders and peers. Even more, I have come to learn from the young activists in my life. They inspire me, challenge my thinking, and make me want to work for a better world for them to inherit. Because of all of these people and what they have taught me, I have taken on my biggest challenge: to write another book! I have learned so much and have so much to share. I hope you will find this work as inspiring and exciting as I do—and will believe, like me, that you, too, can help change the world.

This book will help you see the importance of collective visioning in working together to create a healthy and sustainable world. And it will give you concrete steps for how to do it.

First, in chapter 1, I explain what collective visioning is and how it is done and give you guidelines for how to lead a collective visioning exercise.

In the next three chapters, I give you information about how to build trust and gather a diverse group of people to do collective visioning together. I help you with strategies for how to find the leaders in communities other than your own, how to create a truly welcoming and inclusive space, and how to best prepare people to work together. I offer ideas on how to use personal visions as a way to move toward collective visioning. I explore the power of storytelling in healing divisions and building trust.

In chapter 5, I take a look at how change happens and at ways to develop people's skills and willingness to work together by using different strategies to reach toward the same vision.

In chapter 6, I help you use the collective vision to develop a plan for action.

In chapter 7, I look at ways to sustain work for change in the long haul. I look at cultural shifts around power and positive focus, the broad cultivation of visionary leadership, and strategies for holding the vision and continuing to act while facing setbacks.

Throughout the book, I give you exercises, tools, guidelines, and suggestions for how you and your community can create your own models for change. Feel free to adapt and use what fits for you and your community. Leave out what doesn't.

Visioning is not the only action that creates change, but it is a critical first step. As an activist and organizer for justice, I believe that we have to leave behind many of our old ways of doing things and work collaboratively toward collective vision and action. *Collective Visioning* is an invitation to vision, dream, prepare, and work for a just and sustainable world.

chapter one

How Collective Visioning Works

In a time of great global change, humanity is still relying on the old myth of survival and domination. We need a new myth, a new vision, a new definition of power and leadership. We must go away from the old model and toward one of creative cooperation on our small and threatened planet.

JONETTA COLE

If you can't imagine a better world, you can't create one. If you *can* imagine a better world, you can make one. In order to do this, we have to vision collectively.

Collective visioning happens when a group of people, with guidance, envision a future together. The approach to collective visioning in this book begins with leading people through an individual guided meditation around a theme. The theme can be a very broad question, such as, "What do we want our world or community to look like twenty-five years from now?" Or it can be really specific: "If we could change the media to truly reflect our community and the wishes of ordinary people, what would it look like in ten years?" When I did collective visioning with a group called

Rethink: Kids Rethink New Orleans Schools, we asked. "What should our schools look like so we can feel safe and healthy and have a positive learning environment?"

To me, "visioning" is a verb, something active that people do together as the essential first step of any successful effort to make change. You probably won't find that use of the word in the dictionary, but it comes naturally to me, and it is a common way to talk about this work in my communities. As someone who grew up poor in the rural South and who has been working with others for deep change for decades, I learned early on that it's important for me to use and trust my own language, no matter what the dictionary says. I vision with others to make change, create new possibilities, and bring about justice. I want readers of this book to have everything they need to vision, too.

Visioning helps people move from being stuck in problems to creating solutions. Both expert research and my own experience show that organizations and societies do not flourish without a collective positive vision of the future.

what's the difference between collective visioning and other types of visioning?

Perhaps the most popular type of visioning in this culture is personal visioning, focused only on ideas that benefit individuals and their families. Personal visioning is powerful, but it does not usually lead to collective action. I'll explain more about personal visioning in chapter 3.

A collective vision is not a utopian vision. It is grounded in reality. Grounded, collective vision creates a pathway to power. It keeps us focused on the destination as we travel

together toward it, sometimes with many detours and emergency stops. Some groups may get there in a year or, as I will
tell in one story, more than twenty years. But holding the
vision keeps people inspired and hopeful as they move forward, no matter how many bumps they hit along the way.

Many visioning practices look for a common vision in
which people have full agreement on what the future looks
like. Expecting this level of agreement can be a trigger for
a failed process or at least unnecessary struggles within diverse groups that come together from different places of
power and voice. In my experience working with oppressed
groups and communities, as well as with social change organizations (which often have a culture of critique, debate,
and disagreement), even the word "common," as in "a common vision," can set off tensions and bring negative feelings, especially to those who have often felt silenced within
groups. Sometimes I have used the words "common" and
"shared" (it's important not to get hung up on words), but
I'm always ready to make clear that what I'm talking about
is not total agreement but a vision that many different people are willing to work toward together, often with different
issues and strategies.

Some people sincerely believe that simply because they
say we all have an equal voice, it will happen. But there are
barriers to this goal. First, many people come from backgrounds of poverty, racism, sexism, or other oppression
where they have lost their voices or their power because
they don't fit society norms. Second, without being aware of
it, groups often base their work by default on a culture of
middle-class white people—a culture we learn throughout
our lives in school, in society, and in media. People who

are middle class and white are often unaware that there are different ways of working, so they unintentionally set up meetings that work in ways that exclude others. We need to understand that we have to step out of the status quo if we are going to be inclusive and empowering to everyone. Therefore, we need to create the visioning process in thoughtful, intentional ways so that every person can speak and know he or she will be heard.

In collective visioning, having everyone's ideas and thoughts included from the beginning is critical. Before a group starts to vision together, a lot of work must be done to build trust and agreement so that all participants feel that they have an equal voice.

Only after this trust-building process do the participants begin to look for commonalities and discuss their differences. When individual participants feel heard, seen, and empowered, they are able to begin to look for agreement. More about how to do this is discussed in the next three chapters, especially chapter 2. This prework is a critical difference between collective visioning and other types of visioning.

how to create a collective vision: a starting point

Collective visioning comes more easily to people who come from a "collective" culture, like tribal communities, rural mountain folks, immigrant communities, farmworkers, many spiritual communities, or other communities that are used to taking care of each other and working together. People who are in touch with cultural traditions of art, music making, and storytelling often find collective

visioning invigorating. People who have been in oppressive systems so long that they've given up can have more
difficulty moving to vision, but I find that young people
are especially quick to really get it. I believe that we all have
the ability to contribute to a collective vision, whether it
comes as a life-changing breakthrough, as it does for some
people, or feels like a variation on something that we've
done all of our lives.

People vision in different ways. Letting people know this
ahead of time is very important because some will feel a
sense of failure or anxiety or even protest against the process if they are unable to "see" a vision. Some people will
see concrete outcomes, such as community gardens and
schools, or parks and green energy sources, while others will
see people working cooperatively together and a positive
community spirit. Still others may not experience pictures
at all but have a sense or feeling of well-being or happiness.
Some may "hear" laughter and children playing. All of these
different ways of visioning are important and become part
of the whole vision.

Occasionally, you might run across someone who re-
fuses to vision or loudly proclaims skepticism. In this case,
I usually ask if the person will just be with the others and
stay in the process. Folks like this have their own role to
play and often get very involved during the prioritizing
and planning stage.

Sometimes words can get in the way of visioning. For
example, I recently led a visioning exercise with students
about what schools would look like in five years. I asked
them to draw their visions together. One boy was sitting in
the corner, refusing to participate. When I asked what was

going on for him, he said, "I didn't have a vision. I didn't see a school."

"How did the young people learn?" I asked.

"From people in the community," he said.

"That's a beautiful vision!"

He proceeded to draw it with the collective. It's important to tell people that their visions may be different from those of others. I now say, "If the questions, words, or guidance that we're using in the visioning exercise don't work for you, ignore them. Stay with what you are seeing or feeling in your hearts and minds."

Once everyone has participated in the visualization individually, each person shares his or her part of the vision with the group. The way I most often do this is through having people draw a large collective picture on paper taped to a large table or wall. People who haven't seen a concrete vision are encouraged to depict their feelings as well. Some do this by drawing a group of people (often stick figures) dancing or holding hands, while others draw something as simple as the sun shining, trees, and flowers to depict a feeling of happiness. As folks participate in this exercise collectively, they begin to share and add to each other's pictures. Those who may not be able to draw what they want ask others to help. The creative process of drawing their collective vision becomes a community-building exercise.

leading a visioning exercise

Something magical happens as I watch folks begin to draw together after participating in a collective visioning exercise. One person starts to draw a community school, another person adds to it, drawing a garden in the schoolyard. Another adds a connected elder center where young and old teach and help each other. Someone else starts working on a sustainable energy source, and others join in to add their ideas. All of a sudden, there's excitement as hands reach across each other, expanding on each other's drawings. Those who have drawing skills help others who don't feel they can illustrate what they saw. Other people ask for help on how to attach a picture to the feelings that came up for them. There is laughter and amazement as people begin to see how much they are thinking alike.

This part of collective visioning is only a starting point. The group can now begin to find where their common ground is and work together to take the next steps to build power and make their visions a reality. Visioning doesn't stop with the guided questions or meditation but continues as folks begin to share and exchange ideas. For example, when the young boy who came out of the corner drew a school, marked an X through it, and then drew students learning from people and groups in the community, other students laughed at the idea of no school, but then, after talking, they decided it was a great idea to include community learning in the curriculum, both inside and outside the school walls.

Sharing and exchanging ideas can bring groups together in unexpected ways. At one collective visioning retreat I led, the organizers insisted that I have two separate tables for members who came from two very different communities and cultures. The leaders felt it was essential that the groups vision separately, not only because they came from different communities with different issues, but also because they were immigrants from countries that had once been at war with each other. After a process in which both groups were led in the same guided visioning, they went to different ends of the room to draw their collective visions. Afterward, members of each group shared their visions with the other group. As they explained their drawings, both groups were shocked that the visions were almost identical. They realized that they shared many of the same concerns and that their wishes and hopes for the future were the same. I then explained that even though these drawings were from two different urban immigrant communities, what they had drawn was similar to collective drawings I had witnessed from groups all over the country—from young and old, urban and rural, and different classes and ethnicities.

In every collective vision I lead, people always start by describing the community, even when I ask them to vision about a particular issue. Ideas such as sustainability, clean air and water, alternative energy sources, gardens and local food sources, and joyful people working cooperatively are part of every vision I've seen people participate in. Most often, community art, music, dance, and alternative transportation are included as well. Almost always, technology is a part of people's visions, but as a useful tool, not as a way of replacing community. Always, people are excited and happy over the collective vision they have created, even though they might not agree on every single idea. Of the hundreds of visioning exercises I have led, only once have I had a serious disagreement in a group about the collective vision, and that was over twenty-five years ago. In that situation, younger people and older people divided over a vision of a world with or without technology. As you might guess, older people wanted much less or no technology. The younger people would have nothing to do with that vision.

Often after having drawn their visions, groups go on to create a skit about them. I call these skits commercials so that people understand that they have to be short and to the point while communicating their message. The skits continue the excitement of the visioning and get people to internalize the vision in a different way. They capture the enthusiasm and hopefulness that visioning creates. They also lead to laughter, which pretty much everybody loves. In one skit, a man made little zapping noises and joyfully danced all around the others as they acted out their vision. Afterward the group explained that he was the renewable energy source and networking that the whole community shared. In another skit, each person squatted separately, looking sad and desolate. A man in his eighties entered holding a magic wand and then hopped around and laughed as he touched each person with the wand. As they encountered his magic, they joined in the collective community, showing their good feelings at being part of something bigger than themselves.

Now I'd like to tell you more about Rethink in New Orleans because the story is a beautiful example of how collective visioning leads to inspired action.

rethink, new orleans: just pretend until we make it true

Even among people in extremely tough situations—public school students in New Orleans right after Hurricane Katrina—creating a collective vision and following it up with action leads to amazing results. After the hurricane, several folks who had been involved in working on a remarkable project in Tallulah, Louisiana (I'll tell that story later in the book) came together to do some visioning about "what's next?" Most had lost their homes and offices and were deeply affected by what had happened to their city. What could they do to help rebuild their once-vibrant community?

They decided that there was an opportunity in the rebuilding efforts. The public schools had long been a sore spot in many parts of the city. Because of a lack of funding and other resources, New Orleans had some of the worst schools in the country. The key organizer in envisioning the next steps, Jane Wholey, knew that young people had to be involved in the dreams and decision making about the rebuilding of their schools. Jane lives in New Orleans and I live in Massachusetts, but we have been part of each other's social change communities for more than twenty years.

In the summer of 2006, when most of the families with children returned to the city for the first time after Katrina, Jane engaged her friends in recruiting a group of middle school children and developing a summer program for them. The idea was to challenge the students to envision the schools of their dreams and influence city officials about how to rebuild the schools.

The program was held in a public school building that had been under several feet of water. Despite the cleanup, it was clear that this school had been in deep need of repairs before the flooding. The toilets only half worked, with water almost always covering the bathroom floors. The air conditioning didn't work well at all (in temperatures over

100 degrees daily), and if we did turn it on, it drowned out all of our voices. The cafeteria was shut down, so food had to be brought in from outside. The paved playground, with one basketball hoop, doubled as the parking lot. The line where the floodwater reached was a constant reminder of what had happened.

I was asked to lead the visioning for junior high school students and high school interns for what Jane called Kids Rethink New Orleans Schools. The students soon dubbed themselves the Rethinkers. Before the visioning, I asked the young people to talk about what they loved about their schools before Katrina happened. They had lots to say about what they liked: the culture, the music, certain teachers, other students, and the sense of community.

Then I asked them to get into small groups to talk about what they had wanted to change about their schools before Katrina. The first item that every small group listed was the bathrooms. "What do you want to change about the bathrooms?" I asked.

"Well, we want doors on the stalls, toilets that work, toilet seats, toilet paper, bathroom mirrors, and, oh yeah, soap!" Some told how they always made sure they had enough money to go across the street to Taco Bell to buy a drink so they could use a working toilet.

The second item on their list was books. "What about books?" I asked.

"Well, we want our own textbooks so we don't have to read with others who are slower or faster and so we can take books home to do our homework."

Anthony raised his hand to say he wanted the population to change. When I asked what he meant, he said, "I want there to be only enough kids so that everyone has their own desk and I don't have to sit on the floor." Others quickly chimed in to agree, telling their stories of having to sit on tables or chairs with no writing space.

The next day, we did visioning. All the children had survived Katrina in some way—some at a distance in an unfamiliar town or refugee center, others on rooftops and highway overpasses, some as witnesses of the deaths of family and others; all of them at strange schools for many months. It was understandably hard for them to settle down and pay attention. I asked them to sit down in a circle because we were going to go on a trip, a special adventure. When I told them we were going to travel twenty years into the future, they laughed and groaned about such a stupid idea. But once we got started, the trip we took together in our time machine whooshed us into possibilities that we never would have imagined otherwise.

As we went into the future, I had the students walk around their neighborhood to see what it looked like and think about what they were now doing as young adults. Then I asked them to enter the school they used to go to and see what had changed. What did the entrance look like? The halls? The cafeteria? The bathrooms? And especially the classrooms? Did everything take place in a building, or were classes also held outside? Where? How were the students learning? What kind of people were helping them learn the most? What else was happening at the school that had changed since it was designed by kids?

Then I asked the participants to leave the school and continue on their way to their next adventure. Were they going to work? What were they focused on? As they began to walk, I directed them to go through the park. All of a sudden we noticed something going on at the outdoor stage. The mayor was there ("and she or he used to be a Rethinker—maybe it's you!"). Then the participants heard from the mayor. A young woman in the group, Ardeene Goodridge, stood up. She was wearing a name tag that read "Mayor of New Orleans," and she said, "I can't accept this international award for the best schools in the world by myself. A whole group of us did this together, and many of them are in our audience today. So I would like to share this award by calling each of them up and giving them an award as well." The mayor called each student up to the stage, where she handed each one a beautifully prepared certificate with his or her name on it, thanking the recipient for helping New Orleans create the best schools and teachers in the world. The certificate was signed by the mayor and dated June 14, 2026.

As soon as the beaming, proud students had received their awards, Jane Wholey came running into the room with a microphone, announcing that she was a CNN reporter here to interview these people who, as kids, had created the best schools in the world because they were designed by students and had what students most wanted and needed. Jane interviewed each student, asking, "How did you make this happen? What was your role? And what do you do now?" The students began to talk about designing, building, being architects and teachers, and changing the school culture. These young students' dreams became a reality in their minds and eventually would become a reality in the schools as well.

One student, Isaiah Simms, jumped up, rolled his certificate, and began following Jane, saying, "I'm the cameraman." At the end of the interviews, Jane turned to Isaiah and said, "I just learned that my cameraman was also one of the Rethinkers who were a part of this incredible effort in 2006." Isaiah, in his slow drawl, said, "Well, actually I'm not really a cameraman. I just do that to put a few extra bucks in my pocket. I'm really a veterinarian."

Then it was time for lunch. I told the students they would stay in the year 2026 and that when we returned from lunch they would get to put their visions into drawings and paintings. I was surprised to be met by several kids saying, "But wait! What? How can we have lunch without traveling back to 2006? Don't we have to go back in the time machine?"

I looked at my watch and began trying to explain that we had no time to make the trip back, when Anthony jumped up and said, "But we'll have better lunches in 2026!"

He rushed out the door to the cafeteria across the hall. My heart fell because every day we had been served cold sandwiches or rice and beans that volunteers brought in. But before I could respond, Anthony came running back in, exclaiming, "It worked! It really worked! We're having fried chicken and mashed potatoes!" At first I thought he was kidding, but it was true. A facilitator's dilemma was solved by generous volunteers who had cooked a homemade hot lunch for the students that day.

The young people got so into the reality of the future that when we did prepare to return to the present, the high school students who were working as interns asked if we could please stop the time machine in 2008 so they could watch themselves graduate. So we stopped the time machine in 2008, and the high school students rejoiced in the circle. We all applauded their graduation before continuing our journey back to 2006.

When it was time for the students to put their visions onto paper, a group of young artists called YAYA[1] (Young Aspirations/Young Artists) came in to help. In small groups, the students and YAYA artists designed the bathrooms, library, classrooms, cafeteria, hallways, and outside grounds, which included vegetable gardens and fountains.

Then one young man complained, "This is just pretend."

I explained that he was right—it *was* just pretend unless they came up with a plan on how to make it come true. That was why we did visioning first: to help us see what we wanted in the future so we would know how to create a plan to make it happen. We would start working on that the next day.

At one point during that first summer program, a newspaper article announced that it would take ten years for New Orleans to rebuild the public schools. As the Rethinkers began to realize that this would be after their graduation, Betty Burkes, one of the organizers, asked each of them to bring in a picture of a child in their life—a baby brother, sister, niece, nephew, or cousin—to put on the table of inspiration that always sat in the middle of their circle. This small, beautiful table was filled with messages of hope and encouragement from their elders along with flowers and a candle. Because all of the students held a vision of change for the long term, they realized that the work they were doing might not benefit them personally during their years in school but in the future would benefit children close to them. This understanding helped keep them focused and invested in the effort.

In that first year, the Rethinkers decided to evaluate the post-Katrina schools from the point of view of the students. They developed a report card for every student to use to grade the conditions of their schools. They held a national press conference to present their dreams for the future of their education and unveil their plan to evaluate and report on the conditions of the schools. Not only did every city newspaper and television station cover their story, the Rethinkers were also featured in *Weekly Reader*, in the *Christian Science Monitor*, and on Nickelodeon, the youth television channel. Pretty soon, "rethinking public schools" was regularly repeated in the news about New Orleans.

In the second year of working with the Rethinkers, we led a visioning of what it would mean to build environmentally green schools. The Rethinkers decided to design the bathrooms of their dreams using the concept of green building. With help from an architecture student from the University of California, Berkeley, the students developed a viable design with giant barrels on the school roofs that captured rainwater to flush the toilets. At Rethink's now-annual press conference, Global Green, a national environmental group, stepped forward and offered any New Orleans schools using the Rethink design $75,000 to help build environmentally friendly bathrooms.

Further, after the school superintendent, Paul Vallas, who had just arrived in New Orleans, heard the Rethinkers describe the terrible conditions of their bathrooms, he was so moved that he immediately ordered the repair of 350 school bathrooms. He later made sure that the Rethink green design was made part of the school facilities master plan for the city of New Orleans.

Soon after that, Lona Hankins, the woman hired by the school superintendent to supervise the rebuilding of the New Orleans public schools, called Jane Wholey to say that she had been instructed by the superintendent of schools to work with Rethink, and what did they want her to do? The Rethinkers asked that she come listen to their ideas. Lona has been doing so ever since and has continued to add Rethink school design concepts to new schools as they are built in the city. She is one of the city's biggest Rethink fans. Due to the Rethinkers and Lona's listening to them, every new school built now has hand-washing sinks in the cafeteria, a well-situated garden plot, and outdoor meeting spaces.

The third year, the Rethinkers focused on school food and cafeterias. In the visioning, we focused on the question, "What does it mean to be healthy in mind, body, and soul?" The Rethinkers talked about the kind of food that should be served in the cafeteria, where the food came from, and how the use of local, fresh food not only was healthier but would help local farmers and communities economically. They learned how to design community gardens on the school property and how to offer viable and affordable alternatives to school officials working with a limited budget.

Each year, a new group of Rethinkers enters the circle, and many of the older members become interns and mentors. The first two high school interns that watched themselves graduate in the time machine are now college interns with Rethink. Rethink has grown from a summer program to a year-round organization. A citywide program now includes the Rethink summer school and Rethink after-school clubs at several schools.

Through this process, the Rethinkers have become powerful leaders, spokespersons, lobbyists, and organizers, traveling across the country to speak at an array of social justice events and conferences, including the US Social Forum and Farm to School convocations. At an early age, in the wake of both the destruction of their city and decades of neglect of their schools, these young people are making change real. They have gone on to work on restorative justice issues and continue to work for the rebuilding of schools. Many Rethink students have gone on to become empowered leaders in their own schools and in coalitions around New Orleans. As Isaiah Simms, a senior and still active Rethinker, told the *Christian Science Monitor* in the summer after the storm, "I came to Rethink with a big hole in my heart. Now it is filled."[2]

chapter takeaways

In this chapter, we defined collective visioning, explored how it works, and offered a starting point for creating a collective vision. Here are some points to take away:

- Visioning helps people move from being stuck in problems to creating solutions.
- A collective vision is not utopian but grounded in reality.
- Before a group starts to vision together, work must be done to build trust so that all participants feel that they have an equal voice.
- People vision in different ways.
- Collective visioning is a starting point for groups as they build power and work together to make their visions happen.

exercise 1

The goal of this exercise is to lead a group through the process of creating a collective vision.

Collective Visioning: Imagining a World in 2036*

You can do this exercise with your organization, family, friends, or faith group. I've led a version of this exercise that lasted a whole hour with a weekend to process it. I've also lead a three-minute miniversion. I've led it with as few as three people and as many as five hundred—and once at a commencement speech with students graduating from college. To really do it in the way I describe below you need about two and one-half to three hours to allow for all participants to draw their visions and reflect on them.

In order to do this exercise with a group, you need to choose a facilitator. You can also have a few people to lead the different parts. If you want to be a participant yourself, you can record the visioning exercise first, although I find that people respond better to a live voice. I usually have people sit in a circle and light a candle in the center of the circle for people to focus on if they don't want to close their eyes. Don't worry if one person is distracted or even goes to sleep. Do remember to have people turn off their cell phones. If young people are participating, you might even want to collect their cell phones because of texting. Cell phones tend to be the most distracting issue that comes up during the visioning process.

---

* Add twenty-five to the current year; you can also use one, five, or ten years, or another period.

While I have written a sample script below, I change it depending on who is in the room and how much time I have. I often don't follow my script, making adjustments for the group in the moment. The most difficult issue for facilitators new to this process is the timing. In the beginning, almost everyone moves too fast. For that reason, I have included guidelines for timing.

I start by asking participants to imagine how old they will be in twenty-five years. I ask them to think of a child in their life (their own, a niece, a nephew, a sibling, a cousin, a grandchild, a student, or a friend) and think about how old that child will be in twenty-five years. Thinking of the child helps ground people who have a hard time seeing the future for themselves but can see it through another's eyes. When we visit the future, I usually have the participants talk to the now-grown child and find out what's different for her or him.

Remind people to use the words and questions that work for them during the visioning—not to get stuck on something you might say in the guided meditation. Also, tell them that if they don't see something concrete, note their feelings and any other thing that they might notice. Read slowly, leaving a few seconds between each sentence. Leave about thirty to sixty seconds between each bullet point to allow people time to fully vision and imagine.

In this particular meditation (see others on my website), we travel by using a time machine. The time machine was first added by a young man, Maurice Mitchell, in one of our leadership trainings. I loved it and started using his idea immediately, especially with young people, who are able to vision much better when they imagine physically traveling in time. I have found that adults also respond well to the time machine unless they're part of a very *serious* crowd. Maurice made all the fabulous sound effects. I usually find someone to do the sound effects for me now, but I have also downloaded sound effects onto my IPod. But you can get to the future in any way you wish—for instance, by walking down a hall, going through a door, or using any other way that makes sense to you for your audience.

If you like, play soft meditative music in the background. I like to do this because it helps some people stay more focused and relaxed.

Here is a possible script for the guided meditation:

Take a few deep breaths together and imagine your hearts being connected. Think about your connection to the earth and all living things. Call in spirit, whatever that means to you, whether spiritual being, ancestors, nature, music, poetry, or friends—anything that inspires you or feeds your spirit.

Take some time to imagine a world that you want to live in, that you want children to grow up in. Picture what it would look like, feel like. Think about one hope or seed of hope from this current time that you would like to see grow into fruition in the future.

• Now, imagine stepping into a time machine and turning the dial to the year 2036.

• As you speed through time, know you are headed to a place that is the future of your greatest and most hopeful dreams. As you step out of the time machine, you are aware that we have made tremendous changes and that the seeds you helped plant years ago have now become a reality. Continue creating your vision.

- Imagine stepping out into your community free of any fear or anxiety over your own and your children's safety and security. What would that feel like? What are people doing?

- Imagine having all your needs met. Imagine everyone's needs are met—we have free quality education and health care, and we are working in a safe environment for fair wages. What would be different for you?

- How have human interactions changed? What do you notice that is different as you walk around the community, into the food market, in the park, and on the street?

- Imagine you are living on a clean and cared-for earth—with safe, clean energy sources; pure, clean water for all; locally grown food free of toxic chemicals. What would that look like? Feel like? Smell like?

- Imagine a world in which fairness, honesty, and justice are values shared by everyone, including our institutions, government, and corporations. What do you see in that world?

- Visit with the child who is now an adult in this time. What is he or she doing? What has he or she seen? What is different for this person because of the work we've done to create the current world?

Ask people to spend the next ten minutes in silence imagining what the world looks like in the new future time. You can change the time—five minutes is plenty for children, for example. I usually say, "Spend the next few minutes," then pay attention to when several people start getting restless.

Ask people to look around before leaving and bring one gift, symbol, or memory that they can take back to 2011. As people who have witnessed the future, they return as *ambassadors from the future.* They know what the future can look like, and their job is to help make that future possible.

As they step back into the time machine, turning the dial back to 2011, ask them to think about their experience and what they want to tell people on their return. After a few moments, you can arrive in the current time and ask people to come back to the space they were in before. I usually ask adults to sit for a few moments in silence, journaling or jotting down ideas or images they want to remember, before starting the collective drawing.

Now, tell the participants to draw together what they saw or felt. (In large groups of fifty or more you may want to ask them to get in small groups of four to five people. Or in the case of an auditorium, ask people to share in pairs.) Ask them to share these images and feelings with each other. After everyone is finished, suggest that all participants share their drawings (or if it's a group picture, their part of the drawing) of this future world with each other.

Spend a few minutes in reflection once everyone has shared (I give more detail on this part in chapter 6). Here are some questions to ask:

• What are the similarities, connections, and themes that have arisen out of your collective sharing?

- Do opposing ideas exist?
- How do you feel seeing and hearing about this future world?
- What have you learned?

You'll find more detailed information on leading a collective visioning exercise and different variations for groups, on my website.

chapter two

Laying the Groundwork for Collective Visioning

There is no power greater than a community
discovering what it cares about.
MARGARET WHEATLEY

Designing a collective process that works for everyone involved is a critical first step in creating a successful collective vision for change. To prepare people to work together, you need to understand how to do the prework to build trust and bring together a diverse group; how to create an inclusive, welcoming space; and how to facilitate. These tasks take time and energy, but don't skimp here. The time and effort you put into laying the groundwork makes extraordinary results possible.

prework

First, you need to know whom you want to be a part of this effort. If you already have a diverse group or organization, you won't need to do this step, but if you are starting from the beginning, you need to know how to build your group. If the visioning will be centered around an issue, such as education or the environment, you will be seeking a specific group of people. If you are working at a community level to address people's concerns, then you will be looking for a broader group to represent the community.

To begin, identify the different constituencies within the issue area or community. I have heard many groups declare that they invited everyone, but a certain group, often people of color or poor people, didn't come. Just inviting people is not enough if you are serious about building a diverse group that can make the changes we are talking about.

You need to know what fears, concerns, and expectations participants have when they come into the process. Many people have experienced similar processes that skipped this step. As a result, they have a lot of anger and hurt. Many have also attended meetings during which so many questions or concerns were raised that the meeting agenda was abandoned and the goals were never accomplished. Experiences and feelings like these must be addressed before the visioning process can move on to anything else. You also need to know your participants' cultures, languages, and backgrounds as much as possible.

Be aware that some well-meaning middle-class white folks come into this process thinking that they are there to "help the poor people" or "help the people of color." This often happens because they have been taught that this is their responsibility. Some organizations are devoted to such missions, but for collective visioning to work, as I discussed in chapter 1, it is critical to make sure everyone is equally welcomed into the room and everyone has equal power. This important point bears repeating; none of us can make change without all of us working together. Poor people, middle-class people, wealthy people, white people, and people of color have to work together if we are going to create real change.

Sometimes people assume that if people are poor, they are not smart enough or are too busy trying to survive to work on larger issues. My experience has been totally the opposite. I find that not only do poor people understand the issues on a deep level, but they are willing to spend much of their free time working for change when they feel included, and they know that what they are doing is making a difference.

In bringing a diverse group together, it is important to understand that we all come from different cultures. We may speak differently, learn differently, and understand ideas from different perspectives. This is the joy and power of working together. Often, though, we work in what we've been taught is the "right way"—in which the status quo or the norm is most often a white middle-class way of doing things. This leaves many people out of the process.

One way to bring a diverse group together is to set a goal. I was once asked to speak at a university where my previous book is taught. I agreed to come, but I asked the professor if he and his group would also organize a community visioning day. He was excited about the idea and wanted to reach out to the whole working-class and low-income community near the university. However, he felt that my goal of having 50 percent of the group be people of color might be too challenging. "After all," he said, "this is Iowa!" After we talked about the kind of outreach needed for this process, he went on to organize an all-day collective visioning event of eighty-two people, forty-two of them people of color. It was an amazing event.

A group in Seattle did something similar. Its members brought together a very diverse group by putting white folks on the wait list until half the slots were filled by people of color. It worked out that everyone who wanted to come was able to attend, and many said it was the most diverse experience they had ever had in Seattle. But this didn't just happen by inviting people. It required sitting down with key leaders and helping them become invested from the beginning. Trust and community building has to start before the gathering even begins.

As you decide whom to invite, create a list that is as diverse in race, class, gender, and age as possible. If you are working on one issue, such as education, look for people using different approaches, such as public education, alternative education, and education reform. Or if you are working in a community, look for those who represent different issues.

Before you can bring folks together, you do have to invite them, but there's more to it than sending out an e-mail or a flyer. You need a truly diverse group that is representative of the whole community in a way that reflects the mission of positive change. In other words, you want all the people involved who care about or are affected by the issue at the table. That does not mean you want *everybody* represented. For example, if you were working on an environmental issue in your community, you would invite those being affected and others who care about the environment into the room. You probably wouldn't invite the people who run the industry that is poisoning the community or the elected officials or townspeople who support them. But you would want the people in power, businesspeople and townspeople who support you and want to stop the poisoning of their communities. Think broadly about those who might be impacted. Often, low-income communities are closest to the source of damage. Consider outlying schools, parks, and farms that may also be affected.

These decisions are not always easy to figure out. For example, some people may want a cleaner environment for their children, but their only way of supporting their families is working at the polluting plant. They may not be the first people who come to a meeting, but once you have a vision of how to create jobs for the community as well as a clean environment, those people will more likely join in. In my first organization, the Piedmont Peace Project, many people joined our group even when they knew their jobs might be in jeopardy. And many stayed as strong participants even as they or their family members lost jobs and faced other kinds of threats.

Gather people who care about the same issues, such as environmental change or justice in education, even though they may not be activists and may have very different ways of approaching an issue. For example, when we started a national education network, we had people who worked only for public schools who almost never spoke with people working in alternative schools. But once they agreed that they all wanted quality education for all children, they were able to work together to develop a mission.

Prepare language stating what you are asking folks to come together to do. It can be as simple as "Let's vision

together and create a plan for how to create better conditions in our community" or "What do we ultimately want
to see ourselves accomplish in our work with our faith
group or organization?" And it might be that, as in the story
below, you will have to inspire or even possibly persuade
people about the need to come together despite a history of
distrust or competition.

If you are starting from the very beginning, you should
allow no fewer than eight to twelve weeks to do outreach.
You will need less time if you are working with a community
that is already together and you know whom you're inviting
or if you are starting with a group that already exists.

Find and Recruit the People Who Need to Be There

Recruiting participants can be a challenging and sometimes scary task for people who haven't been involved with
the home communities of all the folks they want in the
room. Almost always, when you are reaching out to a new
group of people, you first need to find the leaders of that
group. Sometimes the leaders are instantly apparent, and
other times they are hard to spot. You may make assumptions about who the leaders are—for instance, a prominent
minister, an elected official, or a self-proclaimed leader.
However, you need to talk to people in the community to
find out whom they see as their leaders. I have found that
often the real leader of a community is an elderly woman
in the neighborhood whom everyone goes to for advice and
who has an open door for the youth.

If people need help in finding a community's leaders,
first I ask them to figure out what the different groups of

people are within their area. An old-fashioned way that I was taught to do this in the '70s and '80s is to go to the yellow pages of the local telephone book. This technique still works today. In the yellow pages, you can learn a lot about who is in your community. Look at the social services section and the church section, and flip through to see what else you can find that tells you something about the community. Look for labor unions and community banks that serve the whole community. We used to use yellow pages in a game to teach organizers how to learn about their communities. They are often surprised, making comments like, "I didn't know we had a church that represented *this* group of people."

When you go to the churches, look for social justice committees, women's groups, or other groups that may work with the community. Ministers can give you this information and may get involved themselves.

At schools, look at who's on school committees. Try to speak to the principal and ask what parents are active in the school. Ask teachers what students are most active and interested in their community or particular issues. Sometimes you'll find liaison people in government positions like the mayor's office or at community health centers whose job is to do outreach into disenfranchised communities. Talk to them about whom they have identified as leaders in particular neighborhoods or within particular groups of people.

The next step is to talk to these leaders and ask them to help you invite folks who should be participating. People who might not respond to you will respond to a leader in their community. You could agree to make visits to the community with the leaders or trust them to prepare and invite a list of people whom they are willing to follow up with. I find it best if the leaders join with the organizer to do the outreach. Be sure to make your expectations known—for example, "I would like ten to twenty people from your community to participate so that every group of people from our city is represented as we work on a collective vision for what we need to do to improve the lives of all of us."

You need to be aware of two things as you begin this outreach. First, many established groups have one or two people who are afraid of bringing in new people, especially people who may be different from the norm of the group. Sometimes these people can be a real stumbling block. I have seen them prevent any kind of outreach beyond their own group. While it can be painful, sometimes these folks may need to leave. In my experience, if that happens, they often come back later. Don't let one person's fears stop the whole process.

Second, be prepared that some people might be unresponsive to your outreach in the beginning. Many oppressed groups have been used and might not trust what you are offering. Remember that often you have to overcome a history of hurt, betrayal, and mistrust. Be prepared to try more than once. My first experience of this situation was when I was living in Charleston in an African American neighborhood. I lived in between the projects and the middle-class black community. As the only white person at the bus stop, I started asking people why our buses always dropped us off at the downtown market, which meant many of us had to walk several blocks into the wealthier communities where most of the jobs were. People were clear on the reason: the rich people wanted black folks to work for them but didn't want the buses coming into their neighborhoods. When I asked how we could change this, everyone would say, "Go talk to Mrs. Clark."

I was nervous but finally timidly went up to her big white house in the African American middle-class neighborhood. Mrs. Clark answered the door, and when I told her that folks at the bus stop had told me I needed to talk to her, she immediately invited me into her house and fed me dinner. Then we talked. I came back several times as we worked on putting a plan together. I talked to all the people at the bus stops and on the buses. Then one day, Mrs. Clark, who was very old at the time and didn't tend to go out at night, asked me to go to the NAACP meeting to present the neighborhood's proposal to extend the bus lines. Off I went, a young, naive, white girl with no idea what NAACP stood for. I returned to report to Mrs. Clark: "They didn't like me, I never got a chance to speak, and they didn't want me there!"

Her calm response was, "Well, of course, they didn't. What did you expect? Now next time you go . . ."

It took three meetings before someone finally approached me and asked me why I was there. When I said Mrs. Clark had sent me, I immediately had the floor. The members enthusiastically embraced our proposal and joined in the fight to take the buses below Broad Street.

Not until later did I learn that Mrs. Clark was quite famous. She asked me to sell tickets for a seat on the bus so we could hire a bus and bus driver to take us all, especially the young people in the neighborhood, to the twentieth anniversary of the famous march on Washington DC, where Martin Luther King made his "I Have a Dream" speech. I had no idea how to begin to sell these tickets. She told me to start with all the lawyers on Broad Street.

I was a secretary in a civil rights law office—one of many law offices on Broad Street. So, of course, I asked the lawyers I worked for first. One of them asked who he would be buying a ticket for, and I said "Mrs. Clark." He asked which Mrs. Clark, and I said "Septima Clark." After that, everyone in the office enthusiastically bought a ticket for her, and I proceeded to sell 120 more tickets for Mrs. Septima Clark, enough to take two buses to Washington. Only then I learned that she was often called the Queen or Grandmother of the Civil Rights Movement. Among many other accomplishments, she had started the Freedom Schools in the South, teaching adults to read and write so they could register to vote, get their driver's licenses, and more.

Talk to People Before They Come

Make sure that you talk to each person you're inviting into the collective visioning process about what to expect. Ask people what questions or concerns they might have, and assure them that their concerns will be addressed before the process starts.

You might want to build a committee of those you've identified as leaders to help do the outreach. Having a committee like this can increase the likelihood of a successful gathering.

People often ask me how to talk to everyone as the group grows in numbers. This task is especially important when you are a national or regional group that doesn't meet often. This task can be accomplished when those who have been a part of the process in the past begin to interview new participants so that everyone is heard from before entering the room. For example, for a Spirit in Action network gathering, six participants from the past gathering did the interviews, each calling five new people. They also helped develop the agenda and facilitate the gathering based on information they collected.

Make sure that everyone's needs are met so that you can have full participation. This might include help with transportation, food, child care, and accessibility. Make sure you identify the accessibility needs beforehand. I have been to meetings where the organizers had hired a signer for the deaf, but no deaf people attended because no outreach had been done to the deaf community. They spent money on something that wasn't needed by the people who attended, but they held the meeting in a place that was inaccessible for wheelchairs. Be reasonable and know your group.

Other concerns are less concrete, but it's still very important to know about them in advance. Some people feel so much hopelessness that they have given up on the possibility of positive change. Some have tried to make change for many years and have become exhausted. Others have heard so many broken promises that they have quit trying. Many other powerful people continue to work to make things better even though they believe "Change will never happen in my lifetime, but I have to keep trying." All of these feelings must be acknowledged before visioning or moving to action can happen. People in the group need a positive focus that's filled with hope for the world they want to live in. Part of what makes this goal possible is thoughtful preparation around the participants' experiences and needs.

As you talk to people in advance, you may realize that some are so stuck in their hopelessness that you need to take a step back and first help them vision for themselves as individuals. This can be a powerful experience that opens them up to the possibility of collective visioning. The next chapter is devoted to personal visioning. However, it's important to remember that personal visioning is only one step toward the bigger goal of collective visioning and creating a different world together.

creating a welcoming and inclusive space

Find a place that is welcoming to everyone. This sounds simple, but here's a story about why it's so important. Back in the '80s, the North Carolina Council on Churches brought in the Piedmont Peace Project for advice on how to create more multiracial participation at its annual gathering. The members worked hard to build the necessary connections and welcome people to the gathering. I suggested choosing an African American church to meet in, but when they checked into it, they realized that these churches weren't big enough to accommodate their large number of participants. So they chose a white church. That was perfectly fine, except they didn't consult anyone local, and the church they chose was (unknown to them) one that a large number of KKK supporters, including the Grand Dragon (the leader), attended. As a result, very few people of color attended the event. The organizers, who were very serious in their outreach plan, didn't understand why they were unable to build the multiracial participation they had worked so hard to achieve.

Knowing the history of a place can be important in many other ways as well. For example, some retreat sites were formerly Native American ritual or burying grounds. Some indoor venues still have balconies that were once restricted to people of color or women. Such issues don't necessarily mean you shouldn't use the space, but if you do, make sure you honor the history. You can do this in several ways, such as telling the history aloud with the group or asking a local Native American person to do a ritual to honor the use of the land and space. I made a huge mistake during one of the first gatherings I organized in my community. I asked people to come to the meeting room at our local library. I had not checked out the space previously and so did not realize that a huge mural on one wall depicted African people as slaves. Please don't make the kind of mistake I did!

If you can't find an ideal space, prepare people ahead of time for any problems.

Prepare the Meeting Space

Because of cost, groups often hold retreats in institutional spaces like religious retreat centers or colleges. When I get to a site, I cover any symbols (like the mural in the library) that might be offensive. If the space is a bare institutional room, I decorate it with beautiful items. I carry a whole suitcase full of gorgeous cloths, large scarves, and attractive print tablecloths. I always put a table in the middle of the space and add flowers, a candle, and other beautiful items. We call this our table of inspiration. You can invite people to bring objects that inspire them to put on the table. Sometimes I bring a bowl of stones or glass or mineral hearts to pass out to each person in our closing ceremony.

Put the chairs in a circle. We always sit in a circle even if our group is so big that we have to put cushions on the floor and build a double circle. We do this because it allows everyone to see each other and gives everyone an equal position. There's no head or foot of the table. The conversation flows better because everyone's speaking to all, not to one leader. There's a different intention to it. People feel accountability to each other when they're sitting in a circle: they are talking with each other, not about each other. They feel a sense of belonging.

Provide Food

Being well and healthily fed makes a huge difference in group gatherings. Depending on the event, you might want to ask people to bring specific items for a potluck. Too many times at potlucks, we've ended up with a lot of chips, multiple varieties of hummus, and drinks. Don't rely on people to know without being told that they should bring a protein, vegetable, salad, vegetarian entree, or dessert. If you don't want to ask people to bring specific foods, make sure those dishes are present.

At gatherings that last a few days, make sure that the food is as good and diverse as possible. It's especially important to check with people ahead of time about allergies and special needs. Ask whether they are vegetarian or vegan. Some people offer to bring their own food to meet their needs and that is fine, but they need to know in advance to do that instead of being surprised. I have gone to many gatherings with southern poor folks from my community and found nothing but vegetarian options. These folks not only didn't recognize the food or like it; they felt insulted that people didn't care enough to feed them "real" food. Those who were serving the food believed they were offering a healthy meal and were hurt that people were upset. This experience was reversed when we brought a group of supporters down to visit us in rural North Carolina. I carefully explained to our members that some of these folks were vegetarians and didn't eat meat, so we came up with a menu that included protein, with foods like macaroni and cheese and baked beans. As our members very proudly brought in the food, I was horrified to see baked beans with ham hock and macaroni and cheese with cut-up hot dogs in it. Our members were bringing out their best and wanting to honor our guests, but I hurriedly ran out and got some vegetarian options for our visitors.

Food is important to everyone, but just as important is understanding our different cultures around food. This is not as much of an issue when you're working within a specific community, unless you're crossing class and race lines. When we were planning a get-out-the-vote event in an African American community in North Carolina, the group decided to have a fish fry and serve fish sandwiches. One of our white staff members from another part of the state asked what we should have to put on the sandwiches. People looked at him like he was crazy. Everyone in that community knew you added nothing to a piece of fish but two pieces of sliced bread!

Food can be a major issue in large national gatherings as well. Just make sure that options for everyone are there. In some cases, I have bought foods for people's special needs, knowing that the facility we were using could not provide what participants needed. We made sure that we brought treats and desserts for a group member who was vegan, for example. He said after the retreat that no one had ever been so conscientious about his food needs and told us how it made him feel so much more welcomed.

People sometimes think that attention to food is trivial or too obvious to be worth mentioning. Here's a story about how powerful sharing food can be. When Andrew Young was appointed ambassador to the United Nations by Jimmy Carter, he approached the job as no one else had in the past, using his experience of community building as a minister and a civil rights leader. He made personal visits to all 159 ambassadors, even ones from countries such as Libya and Cuba, which the United States had boycotted in the past. He never conducted negotiations with people until after sharing a meal together. He attributed this approach with breaking down walls, and said, "You know, I didn't get vetoed a single time. It's probably the only three year period in the United Nations when there was no Russian and no Chinese veto."[1] By breaking bread, Andrew Young built community and held a vision of collective action that changed the way the United States was viewed by the world at the time.

facilitation: preparing people for working together

After you have prepared the physical space and know that you'll have plenty of food, you need to provide a space of community and safety for overcoming the divisions, hurts, fears, and history that people bring into the room. Again, keep in mind that people don't enter the visioning process with equal power, no matter how much we and everyone else welcome them or try to create an inclusive space. People who have been living with racism, classism, sexism, or homophobia may not feel equal to those who come from a background of power unless they've done a lot of work on overcoming the issue. Assuring people they are "equal" does not work when they have internalized negative messages for most of their lives. Sometimes people feel silenced. Sometimes they speak from hurt and anger. For myself, I can still feel silenced when I'm in a room full of middle-class intellectuals. I feel invisible because they assume that I'm one of them and that we communicate and think the same way.

People can be made to feel truly welcome in many ways. The annual gatherings of the Progressive Communicators Network (described in the story below) start by welcoming everyone in the room: the parents, the grandparents, the immigrants, and people of color (by naming all of the ethnicities in the room, including white Europeans). The leaders name different issues, different class backgrounds, different ways of knowing, different levels of education, and so forth. At last year's gathering, the staff director, Carolyn Cushing, and one of the leadership team members, Elena Rodriguez, greeted the group by saying "welcome" in many different languages and then asking if anyone had other welcomes to add. They had taken the time to learn each person's background, and Elena had spent much time researching how to say and pronounce "welcome" in the many different languages. It was one of the most beautiful and heartwarming welcomings I had ever experienced, especially after others were invited to add their welcomes and I added my "Hi y'all!" to the mix.

Another way to make everyone feel visible is called Stepping into the Circle (see the exercise at the end of this chapter). This is an exercise that I often use to build trust and acknowledge all the differences in the room.

Create Agreements

Once the welcoming exercise is complete, the next step is to create a set of agreements or values that people want to use to work together. This process can be short or long. In some cases, I have only a few hours for a training or workshop, so I offer up agreements that many people have named consistently over the years and then ask if anyone has more to add. You can close this short version by asking folks if everyone is willing to work with the agreements, and then make sure everyone says yes. If not, ask people what they need to move forward. Maybe it's using different wording or adding something. As a facilitator, you can say, "We don't have full agreement on the point about not breaking into small groups because we come from a variety of cultures, so let's try to be conscious of our different needs and work with both large and small groups. We can raise the issue again if it becomes a problem." In my experience, generally very few problems occur with agreements as the group moves forward, but make sure you keep an eye on them. Sometimes you may need to offer gentle reminders to people to stick to their agreements.

If your group is going to be together for three days or more, or you plan to meet regularly, you can use a different and more powerful process for creating agreements. Ask people to mingle, say their names, and ask each other,

"What do you need from everyone so you can speak your mind with me?" and, "What do you need from us so that you can step into your full power and truth with this group?" Ask people to share quickly and move on to another person they haven't met. This not only builds community but allows people to participate fully in preparing the agreements together. Then ask for the issues that came up in discussion and write them somewhere that all can see. Review the agreements each morning and ask how they are working. Do people feel the group needs to pay more attention to one or to add any others?

When you return to a later gathering, whether it's a month later or a year later, with many of the same people but new folks as well, pull out the earlier agreements and review them. Ask if anyone wants to tweak, add, or highlight any particular agreements. Always make sure that you get everyone to reaffirm the changes.

It's okay to question or clarify agreements people might offer. For example, in middle-class white groups in the Northeast, I often hear, "Do not interrupt others." In my culture from the Appalachian Mountains, however, and in many other cultures, interrupting is a part of engaging with each other.

Agreements often involve a clash of cultural differences (and personality types), and it's very important to notice that and talk about it. We may agree to be aware of both sides and try to meet in the middle. Probably the most important agreement we make is "We all presume good intentions from each other and know that we are all better than our mistakes." Mistakes will happen, and we need a way to talk about them and deal with them in the moment.

This is a significant way that safety is built. I have been in many groups where the participants make a set of agreements and never refer back to them. It's important to go back to them when something difficult comes up and review what we promised each other.

LIST OF COMMON GROUP AGREEMENTS

Following are some of the agreements that have come up often among participants in our workshops. If you feel your group could use this list as a guideline to decide on what people need, you could hand it out and ask folks to use it to create their own agreements. Or, if you're having a short meeting where you have little time to create agreements, you could pick the most important of these agreements for your group and ask people to agree to them and add to them as needed. If you have the time, it is always best to get the participants to create their own agreements, but this list could also serve to guide you on what might be missing.

- Work from your heart.
- Stay present.
- Slow down.
- Listen deeply to yourself and to others. (With practice, both can be done at the same time.)
- Ask questions before making assumptions. (If you assume anything, assume people are well-intentioned. We are all a work in progress.)
- Learn to live with contradictions.
- Practice self-monitoring. (Notice how often, how long you speak and share the time, for example.)

- Acknowledge that we are each responsible for taking care of ourselves.
- Know what triggers you and manage your reactions and responses.
- Ask for help when you need it.
- Be aware that everyone has a choice to act or not to act.
- Realize that if you don't interrupt something that bothers you, you alone are responsible.
- Go directly to a person when an issue concerning that individual comes up for you. (Gossiping is not useful.)
- Practice letting go. (Not everything needs to be processed or fixed.)
- Notice what's going on in the group.
- Practice relationships where power is shared and people are respected.
- Interrupt oppression.
- Learn about our cultural differences—what people value and different ways of doing things.
- Hold yourself and others accountable to the agreements.
- Agree to disagree. (You don't have to agree with everything.)
- Find your voice and make sure there is room for others to find their voices.
- When sharing ideas, "Yes, and . . ." works better than "Yes, but . . ."
- Trust the people who have volunteered to lead, and if you can't, say what's going on for you.
- Appreciate the hard work of each other.
- Laugh and have fun together!

These agreements were adapted from Spirit in Action's *Guide to Working in Diverse Groups* (cocreated by Spirit in Action circle facilitators Pamela Freeman, Paula Cole Jones, Phyllis Labanowski, Linda Stout, and the participants of Spirit in Action's Leadership Program). To order this booklet, go to my website.

Make Sure All Participants Are Sharing Power

Sharing power is especially important in mixed race, gender, and class groups. If another member of the group doesn't bring up this topic in the agreement stage, the facilitator can. Have an agreement about what we call stepping up, stepping back. This means that if you are a person who is used to speaking first or speaking a lot, then we ask you to take a step back and censor yourself. Even with this agreement in place, speakers will often forget, so it is up to the facilitator to remind everyone. For example, before anyone speaks a second time, you could say, "I'd like to give folks who haven't spoken yet a chance to speak if they would like to say anything." Then call on people but give them the option to pass. Another way to share power is to go around the circle, allowing people to pass if they have nothing to say. Remember to give time for people to think. For example, I often speak easily and talk out loud as I'm working through a thought, which might change even as I'm talking. Other people process inwardly and need time to think about what they are going to say before speaking. It's important to be aware of different communication styles.

The issue of who gets to speak unfolded very dramatically at a recent gathering of a couple hundred people. A young speaker of color brought up the issue of race within the group, and a very heated, healthy, and powerful debate developed. The only problem was that several white men took the microphone in succession, rushing to the front of the line to speak, some more than once, and giving no one else a chance. I don't think they realized that they were doing that, but I found it very disturbing. I was sitting in front near the line of participants who were waiting to speak, so I got up and walked boldly to the front of the line and took hold of the mike. I announced that while several people had spoken (I didn't need to say "all white"—it was obvious), people of color had been waiting patiently in line to speak. I then handed the microphone to a woman of color who had been waiting for several minutes.

Ask people to speak from their own experience. Remind them not to reframe, edit, or correct another person's way of speaking. Such editing happens often and can cause a negative response or cause people to shut down. Many people don't understand that reframing someone's remarks or correcting their grammar or spelling can be oppressive behavior. There are exceptions. For example, I usually ask how to spell something when I'm writing on a board. But one time, when I was speaking at Harvard Law School, at the end of a well-received speech, one man stood up and said, "I think your presentation and information has been very helpful and useful, but I think you would be a much better speaker if you improved your grammar." I was mortified and wanted to sink into the floor or disappear, but as I gazed out at the crowd, I saw the looks of horror at what the man had said. This unspoken support gave me the courage to respond, "You know, in my community, I speak perfect grammar, and the people in my community would have a hard time understanding you."

Be Aware That We All Learn Differently

People have different ways of communicating and receiving information. Some learn by seeing, others by hearing, and others through actual doing or experiencing. All of these methods need to be included as you lead a group. For more, see "A Quick Guide to Howard Gardner's Multiple Intelligences."

A QUICK GUIDE TO HOWARD GARDNER'S[2] MULTIPLE INTELLIGENCES

Because people have different learning styles, including a variety of activities will help everyone to stay engaged.

- People with verbal-linguistic intelligence are "word smart." They enjoy reading, writing, storytelling, public speaking, journaling, and creative writing, as well as poetry, verbal debate, and humor.
- People with logical-mathematical intelligence are "number and reasoning smart." They enjoy asking questions, clarifying their reasoning, and solving problems, as well as scientific research, data, and logic.
- People with visual-spatial intelligence are "picture smart." They enjoy designing and creating, doodling, working with color, collages, painting, and drawing, as well as guided visualizations, videos, diagrams, and visuals.

- People with bodily-kinesthetic intelligence are "body smart." They enjoy physical movement, hands-on activities, skits, mimes, and sports, as well as role-playing, dancing, and inventing.
- People with musical intelligence are "rhythm smart." They enjoy singing, rapping, using varied pitches and rhythms in speech, and attaching a rhythm to an idea, as well as background music.
- People with interpersonal intelligence are "people smart." They enjoy group projects and discussions, as well as building relationships, telling stories, leading others, interviewing, giving and receiving feedback, teaching each other, and creating time to share feelings.
- People with intrapersonal intelligence are "self-smart." They enjoy working, creating, and brainstorming alone and journaling, as well as clear goals, regular time for self-reflection or spiritual practice, and "cosmic" questions.
- People with naturalist intelligence are "nature smart." They like being surrounded by plants and enjoy meeting outside and in nature, connecting ideas to the rhythms of nature, discovering patterns, eating healthy food, and recycling.

For instance, I always bring a lot of toys such as crayons, pipe cleaners, bendable figures, and squish balls to meetings because studies have shown that many children and adults learn better when they are doing something with their hands. Just make sure that whatever you bring doesn't make noise or cause a distraction to others.

Storytelling to Build Trust

Storytelling is so critical to collective visioning that I have devoted all of chapter 4 to it. As Christina Baldwin says in her book *Storycatcher*, "Something is happening in the power and practice of story: In the midst of overwhelming noise and distraction, the voice of story is calling us to remember our true selves."[3] Telling stories breaks down barriers and builds relationships like no other process I know.

Vary the Group Size

Breaking into small groups is important to facilitate different ways of working together. It also often speeds up the process so you can get more done. Some people will always argue, "We need to stay in the whole group." Usually, they are people who have no problem speaking up in large groups or being heard. At the same time, some people speak out and take leadership only in small groups. Have a mixture of both small and large groups, alternating between keeping the whole group together and breaking down into small groups for particular parts. Of course, if you already have a small group, you don't need to worry about this issue.

Play Games—Act Silly!

It may sound ridiculous, but getting people out of their boxes is one of the quickest ways to build trust and break down barriers. Doing the Hokey Pokey works wonders, not only in making people feel vulnerable (and more open to sharing and listening), but also because games like this get people using both the left and right sides of their brains, making them more creative and open to new experiences.

Also encourage people to use movement and artistic expression in the activities of reporting back to the group. I don't know how many times I've seen someone's report on a small group meeting take almost as much time as the meeting itself. I prefer to ask people to do skits or television commercials (sixty seconds), create a newspaper front page with headlines and story titles, or even a radio ad or infomercial (fifteen seconds) as a way of reporting back from small groups.

Sometimes people say, "Why are we playing this silly game when we have work to do?" When you hear that, you may begin to doubt yourself. You might be scared to push people out of their comfort zones, especially if you're out of your own, too—but keep doing it. At the end of the gathering those same people will say things like "I can't believe how much we've accomplished in such a short time." Building trust is critical to moving forward. I call it going slow in order to go fast. The following story is an example of how going slow builds trust.

from mistrust to power

The Progressive Communicators Network is a successful national network of experts in communication who work to make sure community groups and issue organizations get their voices and messages heard in the media. It began in 2000. When Spirit in Action first started reaching out to people with the idea of building a national network, many were disillusioned and hopeless about the idea. Some said,

"That's been tried many times and never worked." Other people worked in very specific ways and disagreed with other organizations' ways of working: they weren't radical enough; they were too radical; they were working only on reform, not real change; or they were white, racist organizations that worked only with middle-class people.

After listening to each person's fears and concerns, we asked them what their hope or wish would be if all of the barriers didn't exist and we could all work together to really change the world. The ideas they came up with were beautiful, and our next step was to send out a letter to everyone that said, "Here are our visions of what we could accomplish together." Then we listed everyone's concerns and said, "These are the things standing in the way of reaching our vision." We told people we would be calling them back to discuss what kind of agreements or conditions they needed to feel safe so that we could address our concerns and work on our collective vision.

After calling each person, we developed a set of agreements based on what people needed with the idea of editing or affirming the agreements at a group meeting. A couple of the agreements seemed contrary to the idea of creating a network. One such agreement was that members would not share their work or training models. (Some felt that these had been stolen from them in the past without giving due credit.) Another agreement was that the idea of a "network" had to be taken off the table. (Some people were not ready to commit to working with each other in a shared or collective way.)

We created a space that allowed for trust to be built and for people to connect personally, through preparing meals together and storytelling on the first day. The next day, we did a ten-year collective visioning exercise in which we asked the group to imagine that all their efforts had been successful in helping community people create their own messages and change the public's understanding of how justice issues about poverty, education, and the environment affect us all. What would the world look like in that future time? People were surprised by and joyful about their visions and realized they all shared the same overall mission. After lunchtime, participants spontaneously began to share their work and training models with each other. At the end of that second day, one woman said, "I feel we've accomplished more here in two days together than in the past seventeen years I've done this work, and I think we should build a network." A consensus was reached. The Progressive Communicators Network was born.

Today the Progressive Communicators Network has had a major impact around the country, helping groups and communities frame messages about subjects such as the enormous backlash of fear and hatred toward people of Arab descent after the bombing of the Twin Towers on 9/11, the role of race and class after Hurricane Katrina and the flooding in New Orleans, immigration issues, juvenile justice, climate justice, education justice, and, most recently, the Gulf oil spill. Some of the members of the Progressive Communicators Network are currently trying to raise money to get a mobile media van to travel around the Gulf coast and help small communities tell their stories. It will continue to be used after the Gulf coast trip for hot spots and disasters.

chapter takeaways

In this chapter, we looked at how to prepare people to work together on a collective vision. Here are some points to take away:

- Leave yourself plenty of time for the prework.
- Gather a diverse group that represents the whole community and reflects the goal of positive change.
- Talk to each person you're inviting into the collective visioning process.
- Create a welcoming space with site selection, circles, food, exercises, and agreements.
- Make sure all participants share power.

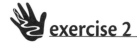

exercise 2

The goal of this exercise is to identify, acknowledge, and honor our differences for deeper understanding of each other and building trust and community.

I use this exercise early on in a gathering.

Stepping into the Circle: Celebrating Our Differences

With all participants standing in a circle, start by calling out specific ethnic, race, class, and cultural identities. Ask participants to voluntarily step into the circle if they believe they fit the identity called out. The group celebrates the people in the center. This can be done silently, by just looking each other in the eyes, or more dynamically by having people say, "We honor you." The first and very important rule of this exercise is to let everyone know that people don't have to self-identify unless they want to. Everyone has the option not to step into the circle.

Say things like "Step into the circle if

- you grew up poor."
- you are over sixty-five."
- you are under twenty."
- you are gay/lesbian/bisexual/transgender/queer."
- your family came to this country against their will" (for example, as slaves or refugees).
- you are of African descent" (and Asian descent, European descent, and so on).
- you are an immigrant or a member of your family's first generation in this country."
- you are disabled."

Name identities you want people to notice. For example, say, "Step into the circle if you are Native American," and point out if no one steps in. This is an important way to honor those voices not present, especially if they are part of your community and should be there.

After naming a few of these identities, ask for suggestions from the group. People often name identities they have in common or one you might have missed. For instance, they may ask people to step into the circle if they are a parent or grandparent, love dogs, love to dance, and so on. I personally like to add, "Step into the circle if you don't have a college education," and am very often the only one, or one of two, in the room when it's a group of activists. It's important for me to do that because I tend to feel bad about myself when people assume that everyone in the room has a college degree. This way I take power in who I am, rather than secretly harboring shame. It also supports others who might have the same feelings, especially when the leader steps in with them.

End the exercise with a debriefing and a chance for people to express any feelings that come up. Ask, "How did that feel for you?" You can ask people to do this in pairs or, if time permits, in larger groups. It's important to ask the question because it can bring up heavy feelings for some people. I have used this exercise in many gatherings and feel it is a powerful way for people to be acknowledged in both their differences and commonalities. But most of all, it is another way to build trust and community.

This exercise can take a half hour to one hour, depending on how large your group is, how much people contribute, and how much time you need for debriefing. You can keep the debriefing short, and say you're taking one more suggestion if you need to end by a certain time.

chapter three

Personal Visions

Shared visions emerge from personal visions.
This is how they derive their energy and how
they foster commitment.

PETER SENGE

If people have never learned to vision for themselves, it's hard to create a collective vision that
leads to change. In some cases, you will sense that the group
you are working with is not ready for collective visioning
because individuals feel so hopeless in their own lives. I
have found this to be true often among urban teenagers and
young adults, especially low-income youth and youth of
color, who face extreme challenges around lack of education
and job opportunities. Such youth are condemned by statis-
tics. They are repeatedly told that a high percentage of them
are not likely to graduate from high school or that they will
end up in jail or dead by age twenty-five. Recently, I heard
an amazing eighteen-year-old speaker, Mathew Davis, say,

> I remember numerous "inspirational speakers" coming to
> my local community centers to speak to me and groups of
> other young black males and giving speeches about how to
> "make it out." They would come in and spout off a bunch

of facts and stats about how black males aren't supposed to make it to eighteen and at best twenty-five, or the correlation between high school graduation rates and prison rates and how we better straighten up (which means pursue white middle-class interest) and if not, we weren't going to make it out the hood and would end up dead or in jail. Looking back, what I find funniest about these speeches is that they were supposed to inspire me![1]

Young adults in general often have a sense of hopelessness about the future, as even those who are able to graduate from college face a lack of jobs and huge student debt. Often when they are working with social change organizations or in public service, they become cynical or burned out. Many who have gone to college come from an academic culture of critique and have a hard time making the transition to a new way of thinking. If you feel this description applies to a majority of your group, and you sense that people aren't willing or ready to move to collective visioning, then you might have them try personal visioning first.

To determine whether it's important to do personal visioning or not, you might check with key organizers about whether they think their members are ready to do collective visioning. Or you could just pay attention to what people are saying as you talk to everyone before the visioning process begins. In some cases, I have held retreats just for organizers who are on the edge of burnout or who have left or are ready to leave the work for change. The retreats focus on bringing balance and hope back into their lives. They provide a collective process for healing and renewal.

Personal visioning can lead people to a renewed commitment to the work they do. When people have balance in their lives, not only will they be more effective, but they will be healthier and stay in the work for the long haul. Some people who have attended my workshops were working in jobs focused on healing, teaching, or human services after burning out in activist jobs. After being a part of our groups, many have made commitments to return to the work for social change with a new perspective and a different, more positive way to work for change.

If you are planning to do collective visioning with a group or community that you will work with in a long-term capacity, you will get a sense when you start talking to them whether they are ready or not. If the majority of people are hopeless, stuck in old patterns of focusing on the problems more than the solutions, or too overwhelmed to take time to think about the future, you may need to slow down and start with personal visioning.

While this book is primarily about collective visioning, personal visioning can be a powerful tool and lead to collective visioning if used in a way that helps people build power. If personal visioning leads people to feel that they can't vision properly because they haven't yet achieved their goals, it's building shame, not power. Just like collective visioning, personal visioning has to be grounded in the reality of people's current lives yet not restricted by their life circumstances.

In this book, personal visioning is not about getting rich or building up possessions at the expense of the earth and other people. It is for helping you achieve your dreams to work for a better world, to find a job that fulfills your soul, to increase your ability to meet your needs, and to bring more health, beauty, and joy into your life. I don't believe I can "vision away" my multiple sclerosis (MS) to achieve perfect health, as some visioning books suggest, but I do believe I can work toward being healthier and stronger in order to manage my MS and lessen its effects.

To collect more stuff than is essential to live happy, fulfilled lives is to have more than we need. Do I have more than I need? Of course! Most of us do. We live in a society that teaches us consumption. As a poor person growing up, I wished for many things that I now realize do not give me happiness but instead make me part of an ever-growing drain on our precious earth's resources. I never realized the gifts that I got from growing up poor—the gifts of community, reliance on each other, and knowing how to manage in tough times. These are gifts that many people of wealth, as well as many working-class and poor people, never got. That doesn't mean I think being poor is noble or good. All of us have a right to have our basic needs met: healthy food, education, health care, housing, and safety. We all deserve to have clean air and water that doesn't make us sick.

I started visioning when I was very young and continued throughout my life, so when I became an organizer, I needed to include visioning in the work I was doing for social change. I wanted people to believe we could really make a difference if we could imagine what we wanted: what it looked like and smelled like and felt like. When I was little, I lived in a tiny trailer, without water or a bathroom. I started dreaming of living in a house when I was about six and for the rest of my growing-up years would draw and design my future dream house. In my midtwenties, after working two full-time jobs for two years, I was able to make a down payment on a tiny fixer-upper house. Throughout my adult years I continued to move to a little larger house, fix it up, and then move again, until finally, at the age of forty-five, I built the house of my dreams that I designed myself. This was a personal vision, not a magical solution to getting what I wanted. My vision provided me a path that included lots of hard work, determination, and openness to opportunities but also allowed me to stay focused and figure out ways to follow my dream, despite the hardships of poverty, caretaking of a family, disability, and an organizer's salary.

A personal vision, just like a collective vision, has to be inspiring and exciting, but reaching it starts with steps that are realistic and doable. Ask yourself, "What are the small steps I can take tomorrow, next week, next year that will lead me to creating my vision?" For me, it was buying that first small fixer-upper and continuing to build assets until I could build a house of my own design. I didn't "just vision" and get the house of my dreams. I worked hard, and it took forty years to get what I wanted, although there were many rewarding steps (owning a home with running water, for example) along the way. I always held the vision. It changed throughout the years from when I was six to when I was forty-five and had a family and needed a handicapped-accessible home, but many elements from the first vision—like lots of beautiful colors, windows, and plants—were still there.

As I've continued to work in community organizing, helping people vision collectively about creating a better world, my own personal vision has been transformed. I no longer believe that individual gain, even in the form of a house, is the answer to the problems facing us today. In fact, I think it often works against our own best interests. In her book *Bright-Sided*, Barbara Ehrenreich says positive thinking for personal gain has destroyed the American economy. She says that the crisis in the housing market is an example of this.[2] We have often heard that if we just think positively and vision what we want, it can come true. This type of thinking can work sometimes, like it did for me in visioning the home of my dreams. But it requires much more than a vision or positive thinking. It requires creating a plan and working toward the vision, heading toward realistic and tangible goals along the way.

As I look at the world today and fear for what lies ahead of us, my vision of moving back home to North Carolina has changed from an individual vision to a collective vision. I own ten acres of land and had an idea that I would use them to build a house where I could live the rest of my life with my family. But I no longer believe it makes sense to try to do this. One of the reasons I want to return to North Carolina is because I miss the sense of community I grew up with, and I miss working collectively with other poor people to support and care for one another.

So my vision has changed. Now I am working with a group of people who are visioning together to create a community that is sustainable and green and meets all of our needs. It might mean giving up some individual control, but the rewards will be great. We are planning to put my land and house into a nonprofit trust that belongs to the whole community. Five or six houses will be built in a circle surrounding a labyrinth herb garden and fire circle. The result will be a green, sustainable community with our own gardens, orchard, bees, and chickens, but unlike most intentional communities, it will be for a low-income, working-class, multigenerational, and racially diverse group. This is now the community of my dreams because it's a collective dream. We are coming together to vision what we want it to look like while planting an orchard together and preparing for how to support each other in creating our own homes. Some of the people moving into the community have never owned their own homes and, because of their circumstances, had believed that they never would.

Ironically, one of today's best-selling books, *The Secret* by Rhonda Byrne, reflects a nearly universal hunger for positive vision. The book inspires readers to create individual visions and set personal intentions for what they want in their lives.[3] That sounds good, at least superficially, but I find the concepts troubling because they promote a life focus that is isolated, individualistic, and materialistic. Unfortunately, these ideas can also leave people feeling defeated and filled with self-blame. After all, if they don't achieve great financial success, then it must be their own fault because they "allowed" negative thoughts. Rhonda Byrne's new book, *The Power*, the publisher claims, "is the handbook to the greatest power in the universe—the power to have everything you want."[4] To me, that sounds like more of the same. The overwhelming popularity of *The Secret* and similar books motivated me to write a book offering an alternative to this popular focus on individual fulfillment and gain. Ultimately, the most joyful and sustainable fulfillment comes from being part of a community with a vision of collective benefits for all.

It may sound like I'm arguing both for and against personal visioning. While I think personal visioning is necessary, it has to be connected to a larger vision that is collective. For instance, personal visioning often helps those working or preparing to work for change get a clear vision of what they need to be doing in the work. It also helps people who are overwhelmed in their work for change find balance in their lives. I've personally learned to use visioning to help me set goals for myself, both to keep a balance of work and play and to address health and family issues. It allows me to continue to work for change for the long haul and be joyous and energized by the work I do.

The following story shows how personal visions are important to collective visioning.

it started connecting

I spoke to Phyllis Labanowski over the phone in July 2010. When Phyllis participated in a personal visioning exercise, a dream from her youth that she had forgotten came bubbling up. She wanted to study art. "There is an artist in me," she thought, "but I have no idea where the money could come from to go to art school." As she spoke her vision aloud, "it went from an idea in my body to a thought in my head." She began to talk to people for suggestions, advice, and support.

At the same time, she became a facilitator for Spirit in Action and realized the importance of art, music, and dance in collective visioning and the work for change. "As we started leading collective visioning in different leadership trainings, it became very clear . . . there's celebration, and there's art and music and dance," Phyllis said. "It started connecting. My personal vision had a place in this larger collective vision."

Although she had been working for social change for years, she had been doing it in a way that did not bring joy. As she began to work in a different way, leading a program that incorporated collective visioning, "it opened the door to the artist in me." She realized that her personal vision had a place in the collective, linked to the life she had been living of caring about a just world and community, a life of service.

She joined a women's support network with the vision of going to art school. In April 2006, at the age of forty-eight, she visited art schools with her seventy-two-year-old mom. In May she applied to the School of the Museum of Fine Arts in Boston and was accepted in June. She received financial aid and attended the school for four years.

Now, she has begun to use her art to help with social justice messaging. She takes complex messages and presents them in understandable, inspiring ways through the use of text and images.

She also created Water Dances on behalf of the fresh waters of Massachusetts. Working with local community groups, she built battery-operated, illuminated hula hoops for public hoop-dancing events that serve as a gesture of appreciation to the water and teach communities a new connection to water, the sacredness of water, and our responsibility to saving our dwindling clean water supplies.

Phyllis says using art is not an easier path than being an organizer, but it's more deeply connected to her own joy. She says, "The collective visioning gave me a deeply rooted vision for what my personal place was—rooted me in reality and what we were building together. It taught me that we all have a place. Like a cook for the movement, there is a place for all of us, and I found mine."

Phyllis was an organizer who had a personal vision to become an artist, and she's now using her art for creating change. The next story tells about Scherazade, who had a dream of empowering young people and realized through personal visioning that she could use popular music and media to reach her goal.

amplifyme

When I first met Scherazade Daruvalla King, she had a dream to leave her work in international business to create a nonprofit that could meet the needs of young people who wanted to make change. She was a brilliant young woman. I was blown away by her vision, excitement, and belief that she could make something happen.

After she came to our training in 2001, she said, "I had no words before for what I really wanted to do. Spirit in Action helped me create a language to create a cultural shift and begin building a movement."

The visioning she did at the training helped her clarify what she wanted to do. She created a young people's organization that used pop-culture music, spoken word, and video to tell the members' stories and create messages of justice and equality. When I interviewed Scherazade over the phone in July 2010, she was eloquent about the work that her vision has led her to take on:

Our organization, amplifyme, has over the past eight years reached five thousand participants. Thirty to forty thousand people have seen our award-winning videos shown on Netflix and most major television networks. We won the Empowerment Award at the Media That Matters film festival.

As many are tuning out of traditional media for information and public opinion, we have chosen to work with the music, film, and video aspects of pop culture media. They amplify the impact of the individual voice and give the power of dissemination to the people. A song, a film, an image has staying power and can become a permanent part of the culture. By hearing empowering, engaging messages and having opportunities to practice taking action through the creation of your own messages, amplifyme strives to awaken a sense of the important role *you* play in creating positive social change!

Our young people come out of this program using the media and the skills to advance issues they care about in their communities. You can use media as an organizing tool, even if you're not old enough to vote.

The following example of personal visioning also involves using art to create a cultural shift, but it took on an international dimension.

realizing a vision

Pamela Freeman first came to our facilitator training to run a pilot Circle of Change in Philadelphia. Pamela is a cofounder of the Philadelphia Black Women's Health

Project, a longtime activist, and a therapist. She has a private practice and was the head of a counseling unit at Temple University. She went on to become a coleader of the Spirit in Action Circle of Change Leadership program.

I spoke to Pamela in August 2010 just as her long-term personal vision was beginning to come true. As part of her vision, she returned to the idea that she had always wanted to participate in Playback Theatre, a form of improvisational theatre in which audience or group members tell stories from their lives and watch them enacted on the spot. Playback Theatre, an international movement, is sometimes considered a modality of drama therapy. Her interest was not to be an actor but to use theater as a forum for social justice work. She believes that stories change people. She also sees storytelling as a way to work on differences around race and class.

Her personal vision that came up during the visioning exercise was to be able to use Playback Theatre to go to Africa to work on ethnic differences. She has held this vision for many years but never knew how she could make it happen. Then she became known for using Playback Theatre in working on trauma issues and was invited to work in New Orleans after Katrina. Later, she was invited to Taiwan.

After that, she said, "If I can just go to Africa and do this work, then my dream will have been realized. But I have no money. I'm struggling to survive. It's hard to recruit people to Playback School (a training program for those who want to use Playback Theatre). It is two to three weeks of training and lots of money. Even though they raise scholarships to bring them to the United States, many Africans who wanted to come to the Playback School were denied visas to enter this country."

She kept her dream in her mind daily and, finally, an opportunity opened. She was invited to come to Johannesburg, South Africa, to speak at a Drama for Life conference on HIV and social justice. She will be offering a four-day course to teach others how to use Playback Theatre for social change. From there, she is going to Cape Town to use Playback Theatre for intervention in trauma around racial issues.

As I write this story today, Pamela is in South Africa, fulfilling her dream. Being in South Africa and teaching the first part of Playback Theatre was a real honor and joy for her. Her new vision is to help start a Playback School in South Africa for Africans.

Not all personal visions have to be as big or dramatic as Pamela's, but as the next story shows, they can be just as important to the work for change.

a big difference

One woman who came to our activist retreats in September 2005 was Elena Pena, the leader of Companeros de Polk, which is a completely volunteer organization working on justice issues in the members' community. Elena was almost embarrassed to say what her personal vision was. In tears, she said that the issue she was visioning around was something that was holding her back from being able to do her work effectively. This issue had been weighing on her so much that it had affected her gusto, her energy.

Her garage was piled with stuff. She wanted to clean it out and get rid of everything to make it a clean place. She said that it cluttered her mind. She made a plan, with her first step to take place in the following week, on how she would begin clearing out her garage. Some of the community members offered to help.

I later called her to ask if she had followed through on her personal vision. She said that she had cleared out and cleaned her garage. She said, "It gave me relief and helped me be more free with my volunteering and working for the community. If I take care more of myself, I can do things with more freedom. It made a big difference!"

chapter takeaways

In this chapter, we looked at personal visioning and how it relates to collective visioning. Here are some points to take away:

- Personal visioning is not about getting rich or acquiring possessions.
- People need to vision for themselves before they can create a collective vision.
- Personal visioning can lead people to a renewed commitment to their work for change.

 ## exercise 3

The goal of this exercise is to nurture hope by leading people to develop a personal vision for themselves.

Personal Visioning

You can do this vision exercise by yourself, but it works much better with a group. You should allow about two hours for everyone to share and to have adequate time for the interviewing process, which is a critical step. If you don't have a leader to read the meditation for the group, try recording it, reading very slowly and leaving several seconds between each question. I like to use a recording even when I'm with a group so I can participate fully as well. You might want to start with some quiet, meditative music.

Ask the people in the group to take a moment to think about a personal goal or desire they have for themselves that they can concretely articulate. Useful language is "Choose one goal you know you want to achieve and when you hope to achieve it by (as far as you can tell)."

Then ask the participants group to share with each other. If people are struggling because they think their goals are too silly or small, or if they seem to have a lot of emotion around a specific choice, support them to go with the idea that comes up for them most strongly.

Here's a script for the guided meditation.

Close your eyes or look down with soft focus.

Take three breaths (together if with others).

Be aware of your body, the weight of it, the fullness of it, the edges of it.

Now think of the goal you want to achieve and imagine the achievement of the goal seeping into your body starting at the head or growing up from the earth into your legs. Imagine that you have achieved it.

- *How does your body feel?*
- *Has anything changed in your relationships with friends, a partner, family members, coworkers?*
- *How do you feel when you get up in the morning?*
- *How do you feel when you go to bed at night?*
- *What is different for you now that you have achieved your goal?*

After about ten minutes, return to the present time. Ask the participants to draw or journal about their experience of having achieved their goal. Give them about fifteen minutes for this part. Don't stop the process unless you're restricted by time constraints if most people are still drawing or writing at the end of fifteen minutes. However, it's very important to leave enough time for the interview questions below.

Have the participants get in pairs and take turns interviewing each other as if they're in that future time when they have accomplished their visions. (If you are by yourself, answer the questions in writing.) All the participants will be looking back, reflecting on how they succeeded. They will speak from the future about how they achieved their goals, what some of the obstacles were, and how they overcame them. Remind everyone to stay in the future time.

Ask the following questions:
- *So what have you achieved?*
- *How did you do it?*
- *Who helped you? How? When?*
- *What were the barriers and how did you overcome them?*

- *What has changed for you since you achieved this goal?*
- *What else would you like to tell us?*
- *What was the first thing you did after the first visioning session you had when you made this goal?*
- *Who was the first person you turned to for support on your journey?*

For a more detailed and expanded version of this exercise, interview forms, and leaders' guidance, go to my website and click on Collective Visioning Exercises.

chapter four

Storytelling to Build Trust and Community

Standing in my power, affirming self in stories. . . .
Shifting mind states, I conceive new narratives
seeing clearly, singing boldly:
I am the change I've been waiting for.

TAIJ KUMARIE MOTEELALL

One of the key first steps in the deep work of collective visioning is storytelling. This is because, for many people, the hopelessness, anger, and hurt they may have experienced in the past gets in the way of visioning; these feelings have to be acknowledged and healing needs to occur. In the last chapter, we saw how personal visioning can help people prepare for collective visioning. Storytelling is a powerful way to do that, too.

Why is storytelling so important to visioning? Visioning is a form of storytelling—creating a story of the future we want. Our own stories ground us in the present while empowering and motivating us or, in some cases, providing healing and connection. Unless we connect with our own stories and truly listen to those of others, we won't be able to vision collectively into the future.

In the process of telling our stories, a form of emotional release happens. Asking people to tell stories can lead them to a place of self-reflection and create a deep feeling of kinship and love for self and others, culminating in a joy that feeds the soul. Telling our own stories not only empowers us personally but empowers others around us, too. It builds understanding and trust. It breaks down barriers between people of different races, classes, genders, and cultures.

I often begin the visioning process with questions that lead people to stories. For instance, I might say to a group,

Recall two or three of the most positive changes for justice and equality you have witnessed in your lifetime.
- What were the circumstances of each change?
- How did the change affect your life?
- What were the conditions that contributed to making that change possible?

QUESTIONS TO START TELLING STORIES ABOUT SPECIFIC ISSUES

These suggestions for questions are adapted from Spirit in Action's *Facilitating Circles of Change Curriculum Guide*, which is based on Appreciative Inquiry methodology.

Questions About Spirit
Spirit in Action believes that to build a transformative movement we need both spirit and action as part of our

work. We define spirit as connection to wholeness, connections to each other, to the earth, and to something bigger than our individual selves. We define action as any act that moves us toward creating a more just and safe world for the future.

Remember an experience where feelings of spirit or heart motivated you to act for justice:

- What were the circumstances?
- What conditions allowed you to act on these feelings?
- What impact did these feelings have on the action?
- What were the ripple effects on you? On others?

Questions About Healing Divisions: Drawing on the Strength of Our Diversity

Remember a time when you were part of a diverse group that really benefited from its diversity:

- How did you provide space for each other's unique gifts to emerge?
- What was special about what this group achieved?
- What allowed the group to be successful?

Remember a time when you were stretched by a different perspective or challenged to change your worldview:

- What motivated you or allowed you to be open to this new way of seeing?
- How has this changed you?

Recall a time when you pushed yourself out of your comfort zone to spend time or collaborate with someone who was unlike you and you felt good about it:

- What helped you do it?
- What did you learn?

Questions About Hope

Remember a time in your life when you experienced hope in the face of opposition or hopelessness:

- What were the circumstances?
- How did you feel?
- What or who helped you feel hopeful?
- Who or what helped you sustain your sense of hope?

A lot of evidence around us suggests that things are changing, if only we see them:

- What signs of hope for justice, equality, and peace have you experienced or observed recently?
- What about this gives you hope?

Questions About a Call to Action

Recall two or three of the most positive changes for justice and equality you have witnessed in your lifetime:

- What were the circumstances of each change?
- How did the change affect your life?
- What were the conditions that contributed to making that change possible?

Remember a time when you were part of creating positive change:

- What was happening?
- What was your role?
- What gave you the courage to act when you sensed something was wrong?
- What are the unique gifts that you bring to making the world a better place?

Think about all the events and trends in the world today and the current response of organizations working for change:

- What do you see as most positive?
- What is having the greatest capacity to effect sustained and positive change in the world as we know it?
- What should we be doing more of?
- What should we be doing differently?

Spirit in Action's *Facilitating Circles of Change Curriculum Guide* was produced by Spirit in Action, with the collective efforts of Circle of Change facilitators Betty Burkes, Carolyn Cushing, Richard Ford, Cathy Hoffman, Phyllis Labanowski, Bethsaida Ruiz, Linda Stout, and Megan Voorhees. To order the guide, go to my website.

I discovered the power of storytelling in my work for change in desperation when I first started organizing in the rural Piedmont area of North Carolina. It was the first time that blacks and whites had come together outside of the textile mills where they worked. I struggled with how to break down the distrust and sometimes hostility that existed between the two groups. At one of our first meetings, blacks and whites sat on opposite sides of the room, staring at each other uncomfortably. Then I asked people to tell their stories of why they were there by talking about their concerns for their children and their future. As people began to tell their stories, the room erupted in excitement and loud voices.

People openly expressed surprise that they shared the same concerns. Telling our personal stories became a process that we used to build one of the most effective multiracial organizations in the Southeast at the time.

In some cultures, storytelling is part of everyday life. Many families in the rural South pass down their histories this way.

Storytelling is a basic human instinct, but so many people have lost that part of themselves. Radio, television, the Internet, and the way we live our lives leave us with no time or space for storytelling. That means losing an important part of our culture. While storytelling is still part of family gatherings and rituals in many indigenous and immigrant communities, as a whole it is a lost art. I find that when I bring people together and they have a chance to tell their own stories, a huge shift begins to take place in the group. New understandings of each other emerge. Many people have forgotten the stories they find buried deep in their hearts once they are given the time and encouragement to tell their personal stories. Many are moved to tears.

Here's an example of what I've seen storytelling do. In North Carolina, we used to have an annual celebration to which we invited supporters from other parts of the country. Folks who supported us often wanted to visit to see our work, which took a lot of our time and energy. So, with the help of volunteers from the Boston area, we created the Spring Tours, where we invited folks to join us in celebrating our victories in our communities. A group of between twelve and twenty people would come—often from snowy, cold New England—to our beautiful spring for four full days. We would rent a small bus with a driver for the visitors.

On the first day, we would take them to see the communities we worked in and give them a tour of the textile mills where many of our members worked. On the second day, we would take them to another area two hours down the road. At the end of touring those communities, we'd visit the farm of one of our staff, Jesse Wimberley, and then would have a giant potluck and celebration in one of the communities. Our celebrations included music, song, storytelling, and all-around fun. The next day, the visitors would go to one of the local black churches, where the Piedmont Peace Project Gospel Choir would perform. That afternoon, they would join in another celebration with other communities.

On the last day, the staff, board members, and the visitors would all meet at our office, originally a little house. There, we would spend most of the day telling our life stories. While storytelling was a common experience for most of us in the community, it was often a new experience for our guests, who were all white, middle class or wealthy, and highly educated. Together, we would do the Stepping-Stones exercise described at the end of this chapter. It lasted most of the day and was probably the most powerful and healing experience I have ever witnessed across such wide gaps of culture, class, and race.

One year, in reviewing our time together over the previous four days, a young staff member told how he felt when our guests, stopping for the celebration in his small rural community, wanted to make sure that the bus would be locked since they were leaving their belongings there. While some people in the room became defensive, saying that they were from the city, where you locked up everything, one woman admitted that her classism and racism drove her feeling of being unsafe.

She was soon followed by others. It was a huge breakthrough that built trust, although through much pain and tears.

Another woman, who fund-raised and volunteered for Piedmont Peace Project and helped organize the "Spring Tours," told a story she had never told anyone before. Through her tears she told us that it was her ancestors, the Wallers, who were the owners of slaves and particularly of the slave, Kunta Kinte, renamed "Toby" and described in Alex Haley's famous book *Roots*. As someone who had dedicated her life to peace and social justice, telling her story that held so much pain and guilt for her was a healing process. She experienced forgiveness and acceptance of her whole self—both of who she was now, and where she descended from.

Every spring, after the storytelling process, we asked all the participants to write a letter to themselves about how they were going to use this information to shape their lives in the coming year and what they would accomplish. After they wrote their letters, they sealed them in envelopes and addressed them to themselves; then we collected them to mail them back a year from the date they were written. Several reported back to us later how they were moved to get involved in issues locally and to work for justice in all parts of the country. One man said the experience totally turned around his assumptions and understanding about who poor people were and taught him about the wisdom, hard work, and contributions poor people had to offer to our society. He was a doctor and a Harvard medical professor who later moved his clinical practice to a public hospital. He helped establish a geriatric clinic at an urban senior center that addressed the many needs of the disenfranchised older members of the community.

Telling a story can help people get in touch with their deepest motivation for doing work for change. For example, when Spirit in Action held the first gathering of progressive communicators, we asked them to bring an item that communicated something about themselves and why they did this work. Our idea was to get them to tell the stories that inspired them to do the hard work they do. Thom Clark, one of the men who was coming to the retreat, called me twice to say, "I'm not sure what you mean. What should I bring?" The second time I spoke with him, I asked, "Well, tell me why you do this work."

He answered excitedly, "Because media is the most strategic thing—"

"No," I said, "tell me why you do this work from your heart."

He said, "Well, because I *think* media is the most important—"

I stopped him once more, and said, "No! Tell me why you do this work for low-income nonprofit groups, for little pay, instead of doing this work for IBM."

After a long pause, he answered in a quiet voice, "Well, because I want a better future for my children."

"Great," I said. "Bring a picture of your children and tell that story."

It was a powerful moment for both of us. He later went on to join our leadership committee, and when we asked people who were interested in playing a role in leadership why they wanted to join, he said, "Because the Progressive Communicators Network has changed my life and the way I do my work." He became one of the most active and committed volunteers in the organization at the time.

Many groups and organizations feel it is impossible to take this much time for telling stories or doing visioning. They say, "We have an agenda, a critical issue, and we can't take time for anything else!" My answer to this is we have to take the time. It comes back to my constant motto: "We have to go slow in order to go fast." Over and over again in my thirty years of organizing, I have found that if we do the up-front work of getting people to come from the heart, building trust and commitment to each other, the work of building a community of action not only goes so much faster but grows from a solid foundation that stays together when trouble erupts. When a group has dealt with race and class, the result is often much more positive than in a group that has not dealt with these issues. When setbacks or problems occur, the group is committed to dealing with them.

In the beginning, telling personal stories is critical to creating community. But once that's done, don't assume that it will continue year to year. For one thing, new people are always entering, and the group dynamics might change. We don't always spend time telling our personal stories if the majority of the people in the group know each other. We ask questions like, "What has been your biggest struggle in your work this year and how have you addressed it?" or "What inspires you to keep doing this work, even in hard times?"

more ways to use storytelling

If I'm in a group in which tension is obvious or if something has caused a division in the group, we will pause and tell a story of what's happening for us. When I'm leading retreats, I often carry my bag of elephants. This idea came from Cezanne Hardy, one of our volunteer facilitators who ran a Circle of Change in Seattle. The exercise came from an expression often used in groups that there is "an elephant in the room," meaning that there is something so big or uncomfortable that no one is talking about it. The group is pretending that the "elephant" is invisible. I carry stuffed elephants of all sizes, elephant hand and finger puppets, and some wooden and plastic elephants. Some look real and others look silly. I will throw them into the middle of the room and read an old fable about the blind men and the elephant. It tells a story of six blind men going out to observe an elephant. They each feel a different part—the tail, nose, leg, and so on—and each has a different perspective of what an elephant is. The men argue, and each thinks the others are wrong. In another version of the story, they are told that they are all right and all wrong. They've only seen part of the whole, and as a result they've missed a great opportunity to use the elephant as transportation for their long journey home!

ELEPHANT POEM

> When I first found this poem, I was very hesitant to use it. As a disabled person, I was not completely comfortable using a poem depicting "blindness." But I realized that this poem was written in the 1800s as a fable with a moral that is still very true today. It is a perfect example of what often happens in groups. Several versions have been written, including one by the poet Rumi. The following is one of the most famous versions written in the nineteenth century.

The Blind Men and the Elephant
John Godfrey Saxe (1816–1887)[1]

It was six men of Indostan
To learning much inclined,
Who went to see the Elephant
(Though all of them were blind),
That each by observation
Might satisfy his mind.

The *First* approached the Elephant,
And happening to fall
Against his broad and sturdy side,
At once began to bawl:
"God bless me! but the Elephant
Is very like a WALL!"

The *Second*, feeling of the tusk,
Cried, "Ho, what have we here,
So very round and smooth and sharp?
To me 'tis mighty clear
This wonder of an Elephant
Is very like a SPEAR!"

The *Third* approached the animal,
And happening to take
The squirming trunk within his hands,
Thus boldly up and spake:
"I see," quoth he, "the Elephant
Is very like a SNAKE!"

The *Fourth* reached out an eager hand,
And felt about the knee

"What most this wondrous beast is like
Is mighty plain," quoth he:
"'Tis clear enough the Elephant
Is very like a TREE!"

The *Fifth*, who chanced to touch the ear,
Said: "E'en the blindest man
Can tell what this resembles most;
Deny the fact who can,
This marvel of an Elephant
Is very like a FAN!"

The *Sixth* no sooner had begun
About the beast to grope,
Than seizing on the swinging tail
That fell within his scope,
"I see," quoth he, "the Elephant
Is very like a ROPE!"

And so these men of Indostan
Disputed loud and long,
Each in his own opinion
Exceeding stiff and strong,
Though each was partly in the right,
And all were in the wrong!

I hope someone who reads this will write a modern version that is not focused on blindness and I will post it on
my website. A kid's book called *The Blind Men and the
Elephant* tells this in a story form that I like as well. It is
included in the resource list.

After I read the fable, I ask each person in the group to choose an elephant. I ask the question, "What is the elephant in the room for you? What is the unsaid thing that is happening for you?" While some laugh at picking out an elephant, just the fact of having something to hold seems to break some of the tension. One person used a puppet to tell the pain she was feeling. She later said it gave her the courage she might not have had to say what was real for her. As people tell their stories in these situations, often both speakers and listeners let go of assumptions as pain and truth come to the surface. Only then can the problem be resolved in a truthful and clear way—not just swept under the carpet. Forgiveness, understanding, and healing can take place.

Storytelling can be used in so many ways to solve problems, build trust, and create a true, honest, and loving community. For example, at one of our network gatherings, people felt one presenter was using racist and classist images in her workshop. Because there was a choice of three workshops, only part of the group saw this presenter, yet other people had heard about the problem and wanted to know what had happened. It caused many hard feelings, so the leadership group met during the break to decide what to do. We decided to acknowledge the problem and to ask the group if we could move on. One of the participants asked to know the details of what had happened. After a few moments, two of us volunteered to stand up and say what had happened and how it made us feel: myself, a white woman who came from poverty, and Anasa Troutman, a woman of color. We each told our story of the workshop. We then asked if people felt a need to speak or raise more questions at that time. No one did, so one of our leaders, Chris Rabb,

led us in a movement exercise that allowed us to acknowledge our feelings, notice and see each person, and release
negative energy. The woman who had led the controversial workshop was present and heard what was said. She
later checked in with lots of people and told us that she has
changed her training as a result.

The next day, we asked the participants to get into small
groups and discuss the question, "How can we work to be
an antiracist organization?" A majority of people said, "We
already are" and went on to talk about how we handled
the problem the day before. That was an example of holding up truth in a loving, powerful way without attacking or
hurting those who were responsible for the difficult feelings.
We cannot get rid of racism, classism, or other isms. They
will always be present, but we can lovingly hold each other
accountable and deal with the issues, not ignore them. That
is what a healthy, strong organization needs to do. In this
case, telling the stories of our own experiences of the workshop helped us get there.

Here are a few more examples of times when I've been
inspired by storytelling and felt it inspire others.

stories and transformation

Like many people who grew up in poverty in this country,
I had a lot of embarrassment and shame about my background. Not until after I had spent time in Nicaragua,
where people understood poverty in a very different way
than US citizens, did I decide to "come out of the closet"
as a poor person back home. Hearing my story around this
country has empowered many others who have experienced

that shame to also tell their stories. After hearing me speak in a large auditorium at the Rhode Island College of Social Work, one student stood up and said I had inspired her to tell her fellow students that she, like me, also came from poverty and had been afraid of sharing that. Hearing my story gave her the courage to share her own story. One after another, students stood up and told of the amazing release it gave them to be given permission to tell their stories and of the shame that kept them from sharing who they really were. When there was time for only one more comment, the last student stood up and, in tears, told her story of growing up rich and her fear and shame about sharing who she was with her fellow classmates.

In another example, I remember once being asked by a friend to pinch-hit at the last minute for a missing trainer at a New England Imagine conference for nonviolent communicators, mediators, and other activists. As I drove to the workshop, I was at a loss for what to do for an hour and a half with this group of experienced communication trainers and consultants. I didn't know what I could possibly offer. I still had no clue as I arrived, and I was asking myself why I had said yes to doing this at all.

Outside the building was a garden filled with small stones. I stopped there and offered a silent prayer for guidance. I then gathered up a bunch of the small, rounded river stones, holding them in my shirt front, and went into the workshop.

I first asked the attendees to talk about listening. They all had advice and clear guidelines for deep listening— something they all did in their work. Then I had them each choose three stones and get into groups of four. Each person was to tell a story of three important milestones in their lives that had brought them to where they were today, while the rest of the group listened.

Afterward, one woman asked if she could keep her stones. She had never told her stories to her husband of thirty-three years and wanted to do this exercise at home with her family. Several others kept their stones as well. I later heard that this last-minute workshop had been a favorite of the conference.

DEEP AND ACTIVE LISTENING GUIDELINES

Active listening to others' stories is as important as telling our own stories. Being heard is critical to building trust. When one person is telling a story, the job of the others is to listen actively, to try to understand, and to reflect on what they're hearing. It is usually not okay to interrupt.

Here are a few guidelines for active listening:

- Listen with your ears, of course, but also with your eyes and your hearts.
- Give all of your attention to the person speaking, showing you are listening with eye contact and body language (e.g. nodding when appropriate).
- Do not interrupt, but listen for understanding. If you have a question, wait until the person is done with the story. Sometimes, in the context of the story, your question will get answered.
- Don't make judgments or jump to conclusions. Listen with acceptance and openness.
- Use silence effectively. It is easy to jump in or ask a question when someone stops talking. Unless the speaker

has indicated that he or she is finished, let the silence be there. Give the person telling the story time to pull his or her thoughts together. The person may be struggling with words or feelings of telling something painful or difficult. To interrupt can stop the story from revealing itself.

Sometimes people talk about very difficult subjects that they may have never had the chance to talk about before. I used to tell organizers to slowly count to seventeen after asking a question before jumping in to say anything else. You can provide positive feedback using encouraging eye contact and body language, leaning slightly forward to show you are ready to receive what someone has to say.

chapter takeaways

In this chapter, we looked at the role storytelling plays in collective visioning. Here are some points to take away:
- Visioning is a form of storytelling.
- Storytelling builds trust and breaks down barriers between people.
- Active listening is as important as telling our stories.

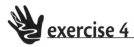 ## exercise 4

The goal of this exercise is to build trust and create community through storytelling and active listening.

Stepping-Stones

This is the exercise that I mentioned in one of the stories above. I have used it for many years. It has been powerful and life changing for many people, although it's probably the most simple exercise I have ever used.

To begin, ask people to get centered, and explain to them the guidelines for being an active listener. (See "Deep and Active Listening Guidelines" above.)

Ask people to tell a story about three to five (depending on time) of the stepping-stones of their lives that brought them to where they are today. This exercise almost always requires ten minutes per person, and some people take longer. Each story is such a powerful expression of self that it's hard to cut people short. I suggest dividing the group into smaller circles if you have more people than can speak for ten minutes each within the time available. You can ring a gentle bell at the end of nine minutes to signal each person to finish up.

This exercise should be done in a very open-ended way, allowing people to take their stories where they want, or if the group is focused on a particular issue, the stories can relate to that issue. In that case, you could ask, "What are the five stepping-stones in your life that brought you into the current work you do for education (or whatever issue you are focusing on)?"

It is critical to allow enough time—at least two minutes per stepping-stone—for people to tell their stories. Each person needs six to ten minutes, so if you have a group of twenty, for instance, this exercise would take about three and a half hours. People can get tired of listening this long and lose focus, so you need to build in breaks, but if you have an agenda, taking up to four hours for this exercise means you might not be able to get to everything else. However, you can ask for fewer stepping-stones. You can even ask, "What *one* life experience brought you to the work you do for change today?"

The other option, which I prefer, is to get folks into smaller groups. Although not everyone gets to hear each other's stories, there is so much power in allowing everyone to tell her or his story in depth and be heard that it's a more empowering experience overall.

For more exercises that are geared to a particular group, focus, or issue, see my website.

chapter five

Same Vision, Different Strategies

The miracle is this: the more we share,
the more we have.
LEONARD NIMOY

Groups usually come together in agreement on a collective vision. But they have a tendency to disagree on the way change happens. People often believe that their own way of working is "the answer." I once believed that, too. But I've come to learn that we need many different approaches to creating change. What is most important to creating the world of our collective vision is that we work together in our different ways—an approach that is collaborative rather than divided.

Starhawk says in her book *Webs of Power*, "Sharing information, sharing skills, supporting the creativity of others, networking, and communicating spread power throughout a group and therefore increase its effectiveness and intelligence."[1]

People come from different experiences and beliefs about how change happens. Understanding how we work for change in diverse ways is important because this difference is where people doing the work for justice and sustainability often split apart. If we look at these diverse ways to see how they complement each other, we can help people connect to their collective hope for the future and affirm each other's ways of working. This can make the difference between a group that grinds to a halt, stuck in frustration and tension, and one that connects to collective hope, drawing on the strength of each approach.

The following model includes four different ways that people think about creating social change. Of course, these four could be broken down into more categories, but I find this model to be the most understandable, and the easiest to work with in groups. The four categories are organizing, reform, alternatives, and consciousness and cultural shifts, as shown in figure 1. I have adapted this theory of change partly using and adding to Joanna Macy's Great Turning theory.[2]

Figure 1 **Theory of Change Circle**

You are probably familiar with *organizing*. Organizing involves bringing together a group of people—either those most affected by an issue or those who feel most passionate about an issue (for example, peace or the environment)— who build power to demand systemic change. We can look at examples like the labor movement, the peace movement, the civil rights movement, economic justice movements, and the environmental justice movement.

Organizing involves building relationships, providing training and education around issues, and mobilizing people to take action. The organizing I have been part of has used a variety of strategies, such as supporting candidates that support our issues and vision; protesting current conditions, usually in large groups; and working for small victories locally that lead to action on larger issues. Organizing also sometimes includes working on elections, lobbying, teaching others how to run for office, and holding elected officials accountable. How much of this kind of organizing is done depends on a group's tax status. Organizations that have tax-exempt status cannot work directly on elections, but they can work on voter registration and get out the vote of their constituency, for example.

Descriptions of organizing can feel abstract or vague without examples from the real world. Here's a story of successful organizing that involved training people to run for office, conducting voter registration, and holding elected officials accountable. As the Piedmont Peace Project was organizing in rural North Carolina and feeling powerless to make change in our communities, we realized that we had to elect representatives who were accountable to us. As members of a nonprofit organization, we were not allowed to work for specific candidates, but we were able to provide training to our members on how to run for office, manage campaigns, lobby, and do nonpartisan voter turnout. As a result, several of our members ran for offices on city and county councils, school boards, and local commissions.

We did voter registration and turned out up to forty-four thousand voters. We didn't tell them how to vote but educated them on the issues. We also worked to hold our local and national elected officials accountable. We educated them, too, not only about our issues but about our power. Our US congressman, Bill Hefner, was a member of the Military Budget Committee, chaired the New Military Construction Subcommittee, and received much of his campaign support from defense companies. Within a five-year period, we shifted his voting record on peace issues going the way we thought it should go from 0 to 83 percent[3] and on social issues that affected poor people from 30 percent to 98 percent[4]—the largest shift in the voting record of one congressperson at the time. Although his principles had not actually shifted, Congressman Hefner knew we held the power that determined his election.

A second way people work for change that often overlaps with organizing is working for *reform,* or as Joanna Macy refers to it, "holding actions."[5] Reform involves changing laws and policies or, in many cases, trying to protect current policies that serve the public. Reform is often a compromise position, but it is critical to keeping situations from getting worse while we work on changing overall systems. This kind of change can also involve politics and the election of people who will support our interests. Some examples of reform that organizers are involved in are campaign reform, media reform, and energy policies.

The compromise that is so often at the heart of reform work can be very hard for people working for social change. An organizer who had worked very hard to get the health-care bill passed in 2010 told me he would have preferred that the "watered down, weaker bill" that finally passed had not passed at all. I agreed I would have liked a stronger bill without all of the attached changes. On the other hand, I could not move back home to a state that did not have a law requiring insurance companies to cover "preexisting" conditions or not to drop people when they got too sick. Now I have the opportunity to go back home to live.

Another area included in this category that all of us are familiar with is providing support and assistance to people, usually referred to as human services. In the context of social change, I think of human services as people holding their fingers in the dike so things don't get worse. This can involve volunteering to feed the hungry, helping at homeless shelters, or doing paid work in nonprofit human service organizations. Providing services and help to people in need is a critical and necessary part of the work for change. The fact that the United States is a rich country where one out of five children live in poverty and sometimes go hungry makes the urgency of human service work clear.[6]

Sometimes organizers call this the Band-Aid effect because human service work doesn't necessarily address root problems. This way of looking at human service work often causes a split among those working for change. Some people say that we're so busy trying to save the babies drowning in the river, no one is going up the river to stop whoever is throwing them into the river in the first place. While I believe we absolutely must address the root problems, we still need people working to save the drowning babies or the hungry or the homeless at the same time that we address the deeper causes.

Here's an example of reform in providing more human services that not only met an important need for early childhood education but was also a powerful organizing process. The Piedmont Peace Project was asked by a group of African American women in a housing project in Moore County to help them start a Head Start program for their children. They wanted to run the program themselves out of their living rooms and get the community to raise money for supplies. Our organizer, Jesse Wimberley, asked the women if they knew why they didn't already have a Head Start program.

They answered, "Because the county doesn't have the money." They had already asked. We offered to help them if they would first let us assist them in looking at the possibility of the county providing the program. They agreed.

Our first step was having the local folks find out what the laws were about providing the Head Start program. Jesse helped them do their own research, and they found out that Head Start was federally funded. All the county had to do was provide a building and apply for funds. The group went to a county council meeting and asked the county to buy a building—an old building in their community that they could buy for approximately $50,000. The community was willing to work to fix it up. They were devastated when the council informed them that the county could not afford

$50,000 for a building and could not provide running water to the building, and they felt like they had to give up.

Jesse then helped them research the county budget to see how and where one of the wealthiest counties in the state spent its money. Two things stood out right away. First, a new multimillion dollar stadium was being built at a school in one of the wealthy parts of town. Second, a budget of nearly a million dollars was available for decorating the main traffic circle with flowers to see as you entered town during special sports events. Reading this, the people researching were stunned into silence. When I asked why people thought the county didn't want them to have a Head Start program, they could not figure it out, until one elderly man said, "Because then they wouldn't have caddies." In this county, African American people traditionally worked as cooks, caddies, groundskeepers, maids, and laborers.

The group not only turned out most of their community to the next county council meeting to challenge the council about spending a small percentage of the budget for a Head Start program but contacted the press as well. They were victorious!

A third way people often think of making change is through creating *alternatives*: alternative schools and curricula, alternative energy sources, or even alternative economic systems, like towns that have a bartering system or time-sharing. Alternatives are significant for our overall work for change because organizing is often focused on tearing down oppressive and hurtful systems, while policy reform and human services don't always focus on ways to change the overall systems that cause the problems in the first place. Those working on alternatives are creating models and ways that we can do things once we have changed the institutional systems, structures, and laws that we believe cause the problems we are fighting. When the students of Rethink designed New Orleans schools with rain barrels on the roof to collect water to flush the toilets, as well as school grounds with vegetable gardens, green outdoor meeting spaces, and fountains, they were creating alternative models. Alternative working examples provide us with vision, hope, and the knowledge that we can do things another way.

A fourth way people think about making change is through *consciousness and cultural shifts*. Just thinking about a consciousness shift is not enough, and often organizers are wary of this approach because it sounds too new age or pie-in-the-sky. However, before people move to action—before the culture can change—their consciousness, or way of thinking, first needs to change. Changing people's thinking happens through education, media, art and music, experience, feelings, and, sometimes, laws that require them to change the way they're used to doing things. A consciousness shift is a critical part of organizing, whether we call it that or not. For example, in our network gatherings, we begin with building trust, storytelling and creating agreements. Many people are not used to this way of working and some resist it, preferring to do business as usual. However, at the end of three days, these folks look back and say, "Now I understand" or "I can't believe how much we accomplished in such a short time."

At one gathering with a group that had met annually for several years, the place we were meeting in didn't allow burning candles, so we didn't give as much attention as we usually did to making the room beautiful. Participants complained and said it made a huge difference. A shift in expectations had happened, so people expected that their work with us would be in a beautifully decorated space with a table of inspiration, flowers, and a center candle. A gathering without candles never happened again!

Change happens when collective consciousness leads to cultural shifts. It happens when the expression of different thoughts and ideas becomes part of the community. These cultural shifts show up not only in ways of doing things differently but also in art, poetry, and music. Change also comes when people organize, work for reform, and develop alternatives. We need all four ways of working for change, and we need to be able to collaborate across different ways of working to reach a collective vision.

Like many organizers, in the beginning I dismissed most of these ways of creating change. I believed that changing the system through organizing was the only way to address our problems. But I've come to realize that all of these approaches are critical to collective change.

At the center of figure 1 is a circle that brings all of these ways of working together in collective power. Every time I have brought together groups of people from all four quadrants to do visioning, the visions have all been connected—across differences in age, ethnicities, issues, and geographical locations. We don't have to alter the way we have chosen to work for change if our concentration is in one of the quadrants, but we do have to work together, building the power of the collective. Only then do we become more than the sum of all our parts.

Here's a story in which young people use different strategies for change to achieve a small but inspiring victory.

theories of change and junior high bathrooms

As I was explaining this theory of change to young people at Rethink, I worked to help them understand what each term meant. When we got to the topic of a consciousness shift moving to a cultural shift, they had a hard time understanding what I meant. So I asked them, "When you first came here and we asked you to sit in a circle, what did you think?" Many said they didn't understand at first and now sitting in a circle was just what they did. One said, "Even with teachers and adults, it means we're all equal and we all have a voice." Someone else said, "We all can see each other and have better communication." Then I asked them how their consciousness change around sitting in a circle had effected a cultural shift. One young man raised his hand and said, "Well, when we went to visit the school officials, we asked them to sit in a circle." Another time, a large group of Gulf Coast Funders came in to hear from different groups. When it was the Rethinkers' turn to make their presentation, Isaiah, a young participant who had been involved in the group from the beginning, asked everyone to get up and move their chairs into a circle. None of the staff had known he was going to do that.

As we got into political and reform work, we began to talk about lobbying. I told them that kids were the best lobbyists ever because lobbying is about getting people to do what you want. When I asked them how they got their parents to do what they wanted, they excitedly came up with tons of ideas. I said that these were a form of lobbying and pointed out that the new school we were in, where they had worked for welcoming entrances and nice bathrooms with toilet paper and soap, was a result of their lobbying and organizing.

One young woman raised her hand and said, "But the bathroom doesn't have soap or hand towels. They took them down."

I stopped in the middle of the explanation of theories of change to ask, "What does that mean we have to do?"

Some yelled, "Lobby!"

Others yelled, "Action!"

The students created a plan within minutes. The first suggestion was to write a letter to the principal, so a group volunteered to write the letter during a break. Then I asked, "How long do you think it will take the principal to answer your letter?" The group decided that they should hand deliver the letter over the lunch break. By the end of lunch, both soap and paper towels were in the bathroom, which stayed stocked for the remainder of the summer. The principal said that the supplies were removed because some students in the school had been making a mess—for instance, by throwing the towels on the floor instead of in the trash cans. So the Rethink kids started monitoring the bathrooms to make sure they were picked up and kept clean.

chapter takeaways

In this chapter, we looked at different ways people approach creating social change. Here are some points to take away:

- Four ways people think about creating change are through organizing, reform, alternatives, and consciousness and cultural shifts.
- Often divisions exist between people with similar visions over the types of strategies used; we need to see how each strategy can benefit the other.
- We don't have to alter our approach to change, but we do need to work with people who use other approaches.

 **exercise 5**

The goal of this exercise is to break down barriers that stand in the way of people who use different strategies to reach a common goal.

Theories of Change Puzzle

The point of this exercise is to help people see that their different ways of approaching issues are each important and that each plays a role in a collective vision for change. The exercise helps break down the barriers that stand in the way of people who use different strategies to reach a common goal. It usually works best with groups or organizations that have established strategies. This is primarily an exercise for those who use one approach and think other ways of working are less important or even wrong. In a community group, you can adapt the first part of the exercise to explore the ways people might think about using other approaches to achieve their goals.

The exercise takes at least one and a half hours to do properly, depending on how much your group understands and how much more explanation they need about how change happens in each of the four areas. I have explained this exercise quickly to a group of organizers in fifteen minutes, but to do it as described below you will need much more time.

Preparation
Make a five-piece puzzle of the four quadrants and the inner circle (see figure 2) by drawing the quadrants on brightly colored poster paper and attaching them to pieces of foam board with Velcro dots. Because I often write on the quadrants to list examples that fit the issues that a group is working on, after I'm finished with an exercise, I

Figure 2 **Theories of Change Puzzle**

glue another piece of poster board on top of each puzzle piece and use it again. When I don't want to travel with the puzzle, I draw the circle on a large poster, and write the separate categories on separate pieces of paper.

Use the picture or model of the four quadrants and the inner circle to describe the different ways that people think about change. Answer any questions. Some people may see overlap between the different areas. That's okay. Many groups work in more than one area.

As you put up each quadrant, ask people for questions and examples. You might allow for a five-minute discussion of each quadrant. I use drawings to capture the examples. For instance, if you're working on environmental issues, you might draw an urban garden, a windmill, or a solar panel in the alternatives quadrant. For groups that work on some issues within more than one of the categories, especially organizing and reform, you can show this overlap in a slice that crosses quadrant lines. Label the slice by writing a word ("electoral," for example) inside it.

Once you've discussed all four quadrants, ask people to take sticky notes and write down the strategies they use to work for their mission. While they are doing this, put up each of the four quadrants in different areas of the room. Then ask people to put their sticky notes in the quadrant that fits. Some groups' notes will be divided among the different quadrants, while other groups will have all of their notes in one quadrant.

Next, ask people to go to the quadrant where they have put the most notes or to the one that they feel is the most important focus for their group. If people are confused as to where to go, just have them go to the quadrant that interests them most. Once small groups have gathered at each quadrant, give them ten to fifteen minutes to discuss their strategies and why they believe them to be most important.

When the time is up, ask each quadrant group to choose one person to stay as their representative. Have the rest go on to the next quadrant and read what others have written. The representative explains the overall strategies for that quadrant and answers any questions.

When the groups have visited all four quadrants, bring all of the participants back together. Ask them what they learned, especially about the other groups. I am always surprised at how much people learn during this experience and how defenses like "my way or the highway" drop. It is always interesting to note when one area has very little action. For example, if the consciousness shift quadrant has almost no notes, what does that mean for the overall work? Or if hardly any work is being done in alternatives or reform, does the group need to get other folks from those areas into the room?

End by listing the insights and questions that the group needs to further explore as they move into a planning stage.

chapter six _____

Creating a Road Map: Vision to Action

If it can be imagined then surely it can be created, too.
DAVID HICKS

A vision works only if we create a plan for how to accomplish it—a road map to get to our goal. Because we know the place we're moving toward, we have more patience if the road detours or if we encounter flat tires, dead batteries, or other stops and starts as we move toward our vision.

Vision grounds and leads our work for change. However, without action it stays "just pretend," as one of the Rethink kids said. The kind of action that comes out of a collective vision is different from the reactive or defensive action we too often see. It empowers people to have hope and to take action together. It takes people beyond what they might think of if the action is grounded only in current reality. With vision, we tap into intuitive, creative knowledge that allows us to think outside of the box. It allows us to think of new ways of working, create inspired solutions, and be more open to opportunities that arise.

Sometimes people are resistant to making long-term plans because they think doing so locks them into one way of working and does not leave the flexibility to change in the moment. This is not true: we can respond to urgent, unexpected emergency situations while moving toward our vision. I often answer this concern by asking folks to think of the analogy of creating a personal budget. We need to know we have the money for our mortgage or rent, utilities, food, clothing, and so on. But having a budget doesn't mean that we stick to it rigidly. We may decide we need to take an unbudgeted vacation or splurge on a special book or shoes. But by having a budget, we know when we need to juggle or cut back on other expenses because we decided to spend outside of our budget. Creating plans for action works the same way. Of course, sometimes we need to shift in order to respond to a current situation, whether it's a crisis such as the Gulf Oil spill or the loss of a major foundation grant. But it is easier to make critical decisions like this in the context of a long-term strategic plan based on our vision.

When the Piedmont Peace Project created its 1991 plan (based on our longer vision) at the end of 1990, we laid out all of our work for the coming year and created goals and strategies for achieving them. During the last couple of days of our planning retreat, we had to stop and redo the plan because we learned that the bombing of Iraq was coming in January. We knew that the war would affect us disproportionately, since so many in our community served in the military. We changed our year plan over a two-day period, but we were able to do it in such a way that we still accomplished all of our visionary goals for the year, although with a different strategy that responded to the current crisis facing us. Had we not had a vision, goals, or even a plan, we would have responded in a reactive mode, rather than moving forward in a way that helped our group strengthen and grow in an organized way while responding to the critical moment.

celebration

When we work in reaction to an issue rather than with a plan toward a vision, we are on the defensive. Even when we win, we tend to feel overwhelmed by the next battle facing us. Very seldom do we stop and celebrate our victories. Celebrations are a way to keep a vision alive and keep ourselves motivated and connected. For example, at the Piedmont Peace Project, during the first Gulf War, when our members were putting in an intense number of volunteer hours and staff were working many more hours than was healthy, every Friday at 3:30 p.m. (when people got off their jobs at the textile mill), we would celebrate. We would talk about our accomplishments for the week—how we were moving toward our vision. For example, we got six more mills to have Silent Coffee Breaks for Peace or four more truck drivers joined in taking organizing kits to the mills where they delivered our materials. And we were thrilled when *USA Today* reported about the truck drivers organizing Silent Coffee Breaks for Peace throughout the country, even though the paper did not credit what organization was behind it.[1] Then we would turn on music, dance, sing, have refreshments, and party for a couple of hours.

Now when Spirit in Action holds retreats, network gatherings, or trainings, we start every morning and end every day with some type of opening and closing: a song, a poem, a game, check-ins, or sometimes just a word about how we're feeling. Even though our staff and volunteers are scattered across the country, when we have a conference call, we begin with an inspirational opening: a song or poem or guided meditation that connects us before we do personal check-ins. The opening and check-ins might take up to a fourth of our time, but they allow us to get work done with a feeling of commitment, connection, and love for each other. They also allow for a safe space in which we can address problems and concerns so that they don't fester and get larger. Often a concern or fear someone raises gets added to the agenda so the group can address it.

moving from vision to action

After doing the collective visioning exercise described in chapter 1, we have a picture of what we want. What happens next? This is where the rubber hits the road. We begin to break down the vision into a realistic and doable action plan. This might involve a one-day process that gets revisited annually or an ongoing process. Within a single organization or a community, making choices about the length of the process is usually easy and quick. With a larger network of groups that are not geographically near each other or that use different strategies for similar issues, the process may take longer as the groups negotiate how to work together, identify their priorities, and plan how to move forward while holding their collective vision.

Sometimes leaders (especially if you don't see yourself as a strong leader) find it hard to introduce new ideas and ways of working. People may resist the new ways, but the important thing is to stay on track. Some people will be uncomfortable with visioning. They may speak out against it and you may start to doubt yourself. I still do sometimes, and I've been leading visioning processes for over twenty years. The best advice is to trust yourself and ask the group to be willing to try on a new way of working together. Even the people most resistant to this process eventually come around and join in the excitement of focusing on what's working and what's possible.

For help with leadership, refer back to chapter 2, which covers the need to know your group. One or two people may be very outspoken and try to derail the process. It's important to be prepared for that and know how to lovingly and gently move on. Remember that it's not about making one person angry but about doing what's best for the whole.

So what are the steps after visioning and collectively drawing? We explore the vision, give language to the collective vision, set priorities, develop the message, and create a realistic, doable plan.

Explore the Vision

In the first step, the group looks at the collective drawing and talks about it together. Make sure that people don't use negative terms to describe the visions. If you're leading the whole group, you can listen for this. If not, you may want to either give instructions about this to the whole group or prepare small-group facilitators to be aware of this tendency.

For example, if someone says, "No government," you might redirect the person by asking, "What form or system did you see instead of government for collective decision making and providing of services?"

Feel free to explore more deeply if you think a vision has not been thought through. Since the example above frequently comes up, let's spend some time discussing how the vision might be refined. If someone says, "All decisions are made locally," ask the person to say more about that. Also ask the group to respond with what they think about the idea. You might say, "This is a wonderful vision, but how would we protect a minority population if they are in a community where their rights as citizens are being challenged or denied? For instance, what about the case of the Arizona immigration laws that go against our fundamental rights?"

This is when visioning really gets juicy, when our ideals for a better world meet the reality of abuse of power. While you don't want to deny anyone's vision, collective discussion and problem solving is important. To facilitate a discussion about refining the vision that "All decisions are made locally," you can turn to storytelling rather than argument to continue the exploration. I ask for stories from others around this issue, and I tell the following story:

> I grew up in the rural South, where if it were up to local decision makers our schools would not have been integrated. (As it was, that did not happen until 1970.) We were required to take Bible classes from a fundamentalist point of view in every grade. In fact, Bible class was mandatory in my school unless you had a note from your parents giving you permission to be excluded from the class. My parents

offered me that option, but I chose to take the class, even though it put forth ideas that differed from what I had been taught as a Quaker, because I didn't want to face the ridicule or ways of being ostracized that the two Jewish students doing study hall during the Bible classes were subjected to. In these types of cases, government plays an important role in protecting the rights of citizens and freedom of religion. So how do we resolve these kinds of issues with our vision of local government and decision making?

This discussion is usually resolved by reaching some balance between local decision making and the role of government in supporting national guidelines and enforcement of people's rights. This is just one example, but it points to the importance of discussion and, once again, the role that storytelling can play in exploring a vision.

Give Language to the Collective Vision

After we create a collective drawing and discuss it, I ask people to stand back and reflect on what they've drawn. Then I ask them to begin to put words on their drawings. If I'm working with young people or people who prefer the spoken word to writing, I often ask them to say the words, and I write them on the vision drawing. In other cases, I ask people to take small sticky notes and add words or phrases that come to them as they look at the drawing. They can add words to their own drawings and to other people's drawings as well. This is another place for exciting ideas and discussion. People begin to see both issues and possibilities from different perspectives and add to ideas that others have.

In chapter 1, I told the story of the young boy sitting in the corner, not participating as the other students were drawing their visions. Because he hadn't imagined a school building but had instead seen kids learning from people in the neighborhood, he thought he hadn't had a vision. After we talked about it, he was excited about making his idea part of the collective vision. When he explained it to the whole group, the other students couldn't imagine learning outside of an institution. But after discussion about his vision, they came up with an idea to have community learning as part of the curriculum in the schools. They used the words "community learning" for this powerful vision, which he had thought wasn't a vision at all.

Set Priorities

The next step is to prioritize what people think is most important or what they most want to work toward. You can do this in several ways. I like to give people three sticky dots numbered 1, 2, and 3 (or color coded) and have them put the dots on the parts of the vision or language that they most want to focus on. You can also have people write the numbers 1, 2, and 3 on the vision drawing or ask people to raise their hands to vote for their top priorities.

After everyone has put up the dots or numbers, see what priorities have emerged. If a lot of dots are evenly divided among more than three categories, you can decide whether to add a fourth priority to work on. Sometimes it's clear that two issues could be merged. For example, a group had listed a fenced-in park in the city where they could let their children run around free and also a community garden. The group decided to merge the two with a community garden inside the park. In some cases, in the process of discussing the different priorities, a group might change priorities, often when someone clarifies what he or she means by a certain part of the vision. Of course when the planning step begins, it may become clear which part of the vision needs to happen before other work can happen.

On rare occasions, some people might say, "This vision is not for me." They decide for some reason that they do not want to work on this vision at this time. You need to allow that to happen and not try to force people to conform or change everything to meet one person's needs. It's fine if someone decides not to participate, but don't let it stop the group process. I've been a part of groups that were so focused on the one dissenting voice that they lost the collective voice and didn't move forward. If someone isn't ready, be willing to give him or her space. Often, I've seen those people return at a later point.

Develop the Message

After the process of prioritizing what we want to focus on, I tell the participants that they are now ambassadors to the future, having had the privilege to visit and see the future of their dreams. Sometimes we have a short discussion on what it means to be an ambassador to the future and about the honor of bringing this information back to people in the current time. Then I ask them to discuss the collective vision and come to some agreements around priorities. If we have time, my favorite activity (and a favorite for participants) is to break into small groups to develop a message to educate others about the vision priority that most speaks to them.

You will need three or four groups that are roughly the same size. You can have people count off by numbers, forming random groups to create messaging about the whole vision, or you can divide into groups by issue if certain people want to work on green energy and others want to work on schools or community gardens, for example. As the leader, you should make the decision about how the group divides. Everyone will have a different opinion about how to divide the group, and that discussion can take away time from the more valuable process of focusing on the visioning messages.

Have each small group act out the message about its chosen priority from the vision in the form of a sixty-second commercial to let people in the current time know what the future could look like and to persuade them to help work for this future. Not only does this allow the vision to become more concrete in people's minds, but it is the first step to moving toward working for the future. None of us, whether individual, group, or national network, can accomplish this work without involving the majority. A commercial is a good way to start to spread the word.

If you can, have props available for this exercise: play microphones, magic wands, scarves, and so on. If you don't have props, be creative. At a recent Rethink visioning, a student took the foil paper around a potted plant and turned it into a hat to show he was the school principal.

Create a Realistic, Doable Plan

The next and most essential step is to make a realistic and doable plan with a time line that has people taking responsibility to lead different parts. Often our visions are very long term, and we have to break them down into doable pieces, usually a year at a time. For example, Spirit in Action created a thirteen-year vision in 2007. We called it the 2020 vision plan. Each year, we revisit the vision, see what we've accomplished, and plan for the coming year. At the end of this chapter, you'll find two exercises. One is for a longer term vision, and the other includes a form to use in planning each goal chosen for one year (or other time line you decide on).

"Realistic and doable" means that you have the people power to make the plan happen. Having a time line keeps you on track for what you can accomplish in a specific amount of time. For example, who is going to do it? How are we going to do it? When are we going to it? This is a reality check. If there is no "who," then the group needs to start back at the beginning because nothing can happen without people taking on the tasks.

Sometimes our visions are very long term—possibly longer than we had hoped. One community took more than twenty years to accomplish its vision. In the beginning, people there had hoped to reach their vision in three or four years, but each year, they continued to win small victories that moved them forward. Now they are continuing on to even bigger dreams. Here's their story.

the long journey to success

In 1989 the Piedmont Peace Project (PPP) was asked by leaders of the Midway Community Association to help them organize in their community in Moore County for more services. One of several low-income, primarily African American communities in the county, Midway was often referred to as the hole in the donut. Situated in one of the wealthiest counties in the state, it was surrounded by the white community of Aberdeen yet was not part of the city and had no city services. Many people in Midway lived with no running water, sewer, trash pickup, paved roads, or police and fire protection. Over 80 percent of their houses were below living standards.

Leaders in Midway worked tirelessly to get others to believe that they could make changes in their community, but people were losing hope. As the young people got old enough, they moved away. Through a community listening project, a vision emerged that had been a wish for a long time—to be annexed into Aberdeen and receive basic services. Looking for a shorter term step toward that vision that felt doable to the community, the community members identified the need for Dumpsters. Without Dumpsters, people threw their trash and junk in an empty field in the community or buried trash in their yards, causing major health problems, including rat infestation. After four months of working to demand Dumpsters and visiting county commissioners, they won the Dumpsters and were able to involve the community in the cleanup project. After that victory, which few people in the community had believed could happen, they held a celebration in the streets for everyone.

The Midway Community Association then moved on to work for the larger vision to become annexed into Aberdeen so that people could receive the basic services that many of us take for granted. The work community leaders have done there has made Midway and other disenfranchised communities in Moore County a model for similar communities across the country.

In 2009, almost twenty years after Midway got the Dumpsters, the community finally achieved its vision to be annexed.[2] The *New York Times* ran an article about the work in Midway and similar communities and examined issues of wealth, poverty, and exclusionary policies that kept these communities without water or sewer services. This is not a unique problem. To quote The *New York Times*, "The exclusion of minority neighborhoods, sometimes called municipal underbounding, occurs across the country."[3]

Now, not only does Midway have water, sewer, and trash pickup, but after fighting town zoning rules several times, Habitat for Humanity is building twenty-two new homes for families in the field that was once full of trash and junk—the focus of the community's first victory.[4] It is an amazing example of community members holding on to their vision for decades among many setbacks and challenges. And they have only just begun.

chapter takeaways

In this chapter, we learned how to create a realistic, doable plan from a collective vision. Here are some points to take away:

- A collective vision works only if we make a plan for action.
- An action plan grounded in a collective vision takes people beyond defensive thinking.
- Celebrations of small victories inspire people and create momentum that keeps them moving toward their vision.

exercise 6

The goal of this exercise is to produce a creative, broad plan for what is needed to reach your vision.

Collective Vision Tree

Preparation

Draw (or have someone draw) a tree like the one shown in figure 3. If your group is small (ten to twelve people), draw a poster-sized tree. You will need a tree that is approximately six feet tall by four feet wide for a large group of twenty or more. You can find paper rolls that are four feet wide in office supply stores, or you can tape or glue poster paper together to make the size you need.

You will also need markers and sticky notes in four different shapes. I have found shapes like apples, leaves,

Figure 3 **Collective Vision Tree**

hearts, arrows, circles, and blocks. The more variety, the more creative your group will be.

If the group is large, set up four staging areas, at tables, if available. You can have each group work on the first step and then have them do the second, third, and fourth steps. You will have duplicates, but that is good information as well. It is important to let the whole group go through each step in order or people will be confused. If the group is small (fewer than twelve), you can do this exercise all together. I allow about an hour for this exercise (fifteen minutes on each topic). Add more time if you are adding more categories or if you have a large group that takes time to divide up.

Exercise

Create four or five small groups. Each group will address all of the following topics:

1. Specific outcomes
2. Goals
3. Resources and support
4. Values and principles
5. Challenges and barriers to overcome (optional)

Count off people to form four or five groups, depending on whether you include challenges and barriers. Having more than six people in a small group makes it difficult for people to add their voices in a short time.

For each topic, answer the following questions.

1. *Fruit or leaves (specific outcomes):* What are the results or the actual outcomes—the fruit—that we can make

Figure 4 **Collective Vision Tree with Group Outcomes**

grow from our efforts? (Note: If you are doing a one-year vision, you can mention that fruit comes only once a year and you can have new fruit each year, but ask, "What can we make happen this year?")

2. *Branches (goals):* What do we need to do, change, or create to achieve our dream? What actions would we need to take to make these things happen? What action is needed from yourself? From the group? From the community? How do we get people to listen to us? How do we use communications or experts to help us?

3. *Trunk (resources and support):* What kind of support do we need from ourselves, our group, our family, our community, and others to meet our vision? (Be specific. For example, support could be getting public officials to listen, talking to our families and friends about helping, or getting help from other people in the community.) Whose support would everyone need? What kind of communication support? What kind of skills, donations, money, and other resources would be needed?

4. *Roots (values and principles):* What do we care about and how do we want to work together to accomplish our vision? What values do we want to see from others? What does it mean to act as if our vision was already accomplished?

If you wish, you can add a fifth category on challenges and barriers that you need to be aware of as you do this planning. I add these in the form of storm clouds or write the words with arrows pointed at the tree.

Have people write their answers to these questions on the sticky notes and then apply them to the appropriate part of the tree. As the sticky notes are applied to the roots, trunk, branches, and fruit/leaves, you should bunch the ones that are the same or similar.

Next, have people all look at the tree they've created. What questions or comments come up? What are consistent patterns that people notice? What are points of divergence?

Note: If you want to go deeper with this exercise, you can add more steps. Feel free to adapt the exercise for what your group needs. For instance, you could make strategies and actions the leaves and outcomes the fruit. At a recent workshop, our Power Up Networks trainer, Taij Kumarie Moteelall, had people use dead branches to symbolize things we needed to let go of and butterflies for transformation and cultural shifts needed.

exercise 7

The goal of this exercise is to produce a very strategic, time-specific, concrete plan that covers a period of up to one year.

Strategic Short-Term Planning

Make a list of goals, or use a list of vision priorities generated as described in this chapter. Then use the planning form (fig. 5) to create a plan to reach each goal on that list. You can work on the plan with the whole group or break into small groups. However you do it, use these three very important guidelines:

- If you lay out a plan and don't have enough people or leaders to carry it out, then you have to go back and either downsize the plan to make it doable or create a plan to first build up to the number of people you need.
- Make sure you compare all the goals and lay them out on a calendar. You don't want to be planning a fundraiser during another campaign or action, so make sure the plans fit together.
- Ask all participants to take an inventory of their time. If their time is already stretched to the limit, what are they going to give up or shift in order to achieve their vision? You can use creative brainstorming to help people answer this question. For example, at the Piedmont Peace Project, many people had children or elders they needed to care for. We figured out a way to include them. It wasn't unusual for us to have four generations working together on a project.

Leave plenty of time for this exercise in order for groups to come up with a well-thought-out, thorough plan. A minimum would be one and a half hours, but two hours would be preferable.

Figure 5 shows a form I use for planning each goal. You can change the words to fit your group's needs, but having a format for people to work from is very important. Some of my forms are very simple, and some are more complex, depending on the group I'm working with. All have the same basic planning questions. (For a PDF file to download for your group, go to my website.)

GOAL:	
What are the tasks to accomplish for your goal? (List each one separately)	
How will you accomplish each task? What specific steps will you take?	
Who will take the lead on each task? Who else will help? If you do not have enough people, how will you recruit others?	
When will these steps happen by?	
What do you need to make this happen (resources, money, people with expertise, etc.)	
How will you get these resources, and what will you do if you don't have all of them?	

Figure 5 **Strategic Planning Form**

chapter seven

Grounded in Vision for the Long Haul

No problem can be solved from the same
level of consciousness that created it.
We must learn to see the world anew.
ALBERT EINSTEIN

Anyone who has worked for social change for a
few years (or, like me, for decades) has heard stories like the one I told about the nuclear freeze campaign in
the preface: important groups and movements with many
dedicated people working for them passionately become
smaller and less effective—or disappear—over the long
haul. Actually, most of the leaders go on to work in new
or different groups or on different issues. But wouldn't it be
great to have organizations that continue to thrive and grow
in capacity to support social change as our movements swell
and start to achieve our dreams? I believe that we need cultural shifts about power and a positive focus, broad and specific cultivation of visionary leadership, and strategies for
facing setbacks in order to build strong groups that help us
reach our collective visions.

cultural shifts: power and positive focus

In chapter 5, I discussed how shifts in culture and consciousness are a critical way of making change. We also need cultural shifts in how we think about power and how we learn from past experiences. These shifts could strengthen many groups working for change.

Too often, the culture in our work for change includes fear of power and disrespect for leaders because to many people, leadership equals power over us. This whole book has been about how to create a collective vision and move from vision into action, but we can never achieve our dreams as long as we are afraid of gaining our own power.

This fear is understandable, especially among oppressed people. For centuries, power has been used to oppress people and to create divides between those who have power over others and those who don't. But we need to think about power differently: power *with* instead of power *over*. If we are going to make real change in our communities and the broader world, we have to embrace a new kind of power—a power that is equitable and shared. Many times, groups pull back when they think they are getting too powerful. Fear of power keeps them from being able to envision what they really want or need. In my experience, this especially comes up in groups' fears around fund-raising and being able to confront those in power. We even see it in basic struggles about whether they deserve livable wages, benefits, or time to have fun.

While we must learn to embrace power in order to make changes, we also need to hold each other lovingly accountable in that power. We need to support our leaders, even

when they make mistakes, but also have them be accountable to us. When I say "lovingly accountable," I'm not talking about attacking our own leaders, which happens too
often, but about helping them stay on track and remember
that they are our leaders. Especially as we elect our own
people to leadership roles, in government, for example, we
often get angry when they don't do exactly what we want.
But, unfortunately, there is a need, especially in politics, for
compromise and picking our fights.

For example, in the Piedmont Peace Project, our congressman, Bill Hefner, was not one of our own group but
a conservative Democrat in North Carolina. We began to
hold him accountable to us once we built enough power
to affect his election. We didn't push on any votes or bills
that we knew were lost causes, but we let him know that we
weren't pushing because we knew the bill would lose even if
he voted the right way. We allowed him to vote differently
on some issues that were dear to our hearts while we really
pushed on issues we cared about when we knew we had a
chance to win. Even with that strategy, he still became a
target of the political right as his voting record started to
change toward more peace and social justice issues.

I encourage you and your group to learn more about
how to embrace and effectively use power in positive ways
for creating the world we want. Many resources are available on building and sharing power with others (including
doing so with accountability). For more information, see
the resource list at the end of the book.

Another cultural shift that needs to be made in our work
for change is central to the premise of this book: looking
at the positive and focusing on things that are constructive

and affirmative. We often feel guilty about doing that or believe if we are not holding out the problem, we are taking the wrong approach. However, we need to approach problems in a different way. Although we have won many victories by focusing on the negative, we still have not built a large enough base of power to keep moving forward until we have achieved equality, justice, and sustainability for everyone. A focus on the positive is an idea that has been adopted in many socially conscious businesses but has been slow to catch on in our movements for change.

When I started Spirit in Action, we spent several months running Circles of Change throughout the country. I referred to them as experiential grassroots think tanks. We trained leaders to use different ways of working with groups: collective visioning, building community, healing divisions, and inspiring action based on a collective vision. Most of the leaders worked in pairs. They found it helpful to have a partner so that they could plan together, colead, and support each other through the process. After leading these circles over a thirteen-week period during which each leader used a curriculum we had developed, we held a retreat for all the circle leaders. I told the group that, while we would focus on the things that didn't work well or needed improvement or reworking on the second day, our first day together would be about looking at all the things that worked well. I believed that if we started with the positive, we could build on that, so problem solving would be easier to do. I was surprised at the amount of resistance the group had to doing this.

One person said, "If I can't talk about what didn't work, then I don't want to talk about this at all." Immediately another person agreed, and then a third person said, "I want to hear what they have to say." Some people began to nod in agreement. I took a deep breath, gathered my courage, and said, "Well, you have the option not to talk, but I really would like for all of us to hear about what worked in your circle." It was a very difficult thing to do since, as a leader, I was used to listening to the group and responding to their requests and needs. However, in this kind of work, we are going against a culture that is deeply rooted in focusing on problems, not looking at what works. If we are going to do the work of creating a cultural shift in how we work for change, we have to be willing to step out on a limb, make mistakes, and be vulnerable. We also have to hold firm against voices of dissent when we're leaders trying to create a different way of working. Remember, in the situation I just described, I didn't say we would not talk about the critiques and problems—just that the first day would be focused on what worked. Even that brought resistance and discomfort from a few participants.

What I have found is that many people, often those who don't have stronger voices or feel they don't have equal power, are very inspired and excited about this process. For the first time, many people feel their voices are included. This way of working makes them feel empowered. Others who are resistant in the beginning often start to see the value of working in a different way. One of the women who expressed resistance the first day of the retreat said the next day that she was glad we didn't do it the way she had wanted. She expressed her excitement about learning how to work in a different way.

Eventually, when a group begins to accept and appreciate this way of doing things, it becomes part of the culture of the group. As new people enter, they are brought into a different culture. At that point, the whole group takes responsibility for holding the process of positive and affirming leadership.

leadership

In addition to cultural shifts about power and a positive focus, we must be able to mobilize the people to make change happen. We need visionary leadership in order to sustain enough power to change the status quo, whether locally or globally. Leading with vision allows us to change the hearts and minds of others. We become leaders that people follow with hope and excitement.

It is important to understand the role visionary leaders play in society. A good leader is not a person who acts alone or makes decisions alone but someone who is part of a process that includes the voices and ideas of others. For example, none of the ideas I write about here were created in isolation. They came from being in groups, leading groups, and, with every exercise and question, incorporating other people's thoughts, ideas, and feelings. We sometimes think of leaders as having all the answers, but a true and powerful leader knows how to listen deeply and involve and inspire others to also take on leadership and connect to the whole collective vision. A great visionary leader also knows how to move people to concrete action. Here's how to make that happen and what it feels and looks like when it does.

I have already mentioned the role of leadership in shifting the culture and the need to take the actions, make the time, and sustain the effort to allow a new culture to develop. This work is often scary and challenging, which is why we supported our leaders and coached them on a weekly basis when we were starting Circles of Change. It's also why we encourage people to have partners, so that one strong voice of dissent won't get us off track.

Once, when we needed to get a group back on track, I asked my coleader to pull a chair into the middle of the circle with me (this is often referred to as a fishbowl), and we talked out loud to each other about how we felt, why we were trying to create a different atmosphere that empowered everyone, and how we could respond respectfully to those who were used to working in the old ways without losing the ability to try something new. We then invited others to come in and take our chairs to continue the discussion. Because we'd had that discussion openly and transparently, people began to come into the center and talk about how they felt. Some expressed joy and excitement about working differently and talked about how often they had left meetings feeling depleted and disempowered. They said the way we were working gave them hope. Eventually, some of the people with dissenting voices came into the circle and talked about their fear of working differently. They also began to talk about wanting to be open to trying new processes in a way that was more inclusive. We were able to move forward.

At another meeting, one man pantomimed stepping out of a box when he stood up to say something that was out of his comfort zone. It helped him to use humor. He modeled to us a way that used humor to address the discomfort of working in a different way.

After an action plan is created from a collective vision, someone (or a leadership committee) needs to take responsibility for holding the whole vision, weaving the pieces together (for example, the different priorities chosen), motivating people, and keeping them grounded in the agreements and the vision. Too often, groups make plans and people excitedly make commitments. Then they go home, get caught up in their busy lives, and forget about the commitments they made. Other times, people get overwhelmed and don't know where to start. Follow up with folks to keep them excited. This involves meetings, phone calls, e-mails, and reminders.

Just as we honor different learning styles when we do visioning and planning, we also have to accept different ways of working. Some people are great at keeping schedules and fulfilling every commitment they make, while others need folks to remind them, nudge them, and help them stay on track. I often find that when people aren't doing what they said they would, they have gotten stuck and just need to talk about it in order to find the courage to take the next step. This is especially true for people new to this work. Or sometimes what they need is a little support to develop a personal plan for how to do what they need to do.

Also, the ways we use to contact people have to be diverse. Some people respond best to e-mail, others to phone calls, while others need face-to-face visits. As leaders, we need to accept this and not take it personally if people don't respond to a certain message or to the first outreach. And of course, you will always have people who overcommit or, because of family circumstances, emergencies, or health issues, cannot follow through. It's important not to assign blame but to make sure that someone else takes on that person's tasks.

The leaders must take responsibility for organizing the process: setting up monthly phone calls, communication systems, meeting times, and so on. This is a critical role that often gets dropped because people either believe that everyone can share equal leadership or that the role of leaders can shift from person to person. However, not everyone has the personality or skills to be this kind of leader. Having this role doesn't mean that someone has more power than others. Instead, this role is necessary to maintain communications and connections to the different people, committees, and parts of the plan.

Leaders must lead by vision. Be the example of the kind of leader you want to have in your vision of a just world, or as Gandhi said, "You must be the change you want to see in the world."

setback and attacks

As we have seen, a group's long-term survival depends on making shifts around power and a positive focus and supporting visionary leadership. Having strategies for dealing with setbacks is also crucial. Whether our efforts are individual or collective, we often experience setbacks and attacks and other disappointments in our work. But when we're grounded in a long-term vision, we can see these setbacks as ways to learn and continue to move forward instead of giving up or thinking we somehow did something wrong.

The first step after experiencing a loss or what we might think of as a failure is to evaluate what happened. I don't use the traditional type of evaluation: examining only what went wrong. While this is an important part of the process, the first step is to look at what worked and what we learned from the experience. Then it's easier to look at what didn't work and what we can learn from that as well. (This approach may sound familiar by now, but it can be challenging in practice, so it can't be mentioned too often.) It does no good to dwell on what we did wrong unless we also look at how we would do it differently next time. This allows us to constantly learn and change our methods.

In addition, as our communication, technology, and society change, so our work must also change. We need to be prepared to adjust to the needs and changes of our groups, communities, and organizations.

We used to have a guideline for our Piedmont Peace Project weekly staff meetings. We asked each person to say an "appreciate" and then a "concern or complaint." If someone did have a concern or complaint, we asked the person to follow it with suggestions for a solution, even if it was as simple as "We need to meet and talk about this more." This kept people from just complaining or blaming without thinking about being part of the solution.

So not only might we need to address setbacks by doing something different, but we also have to be aware and ready for planned attacks. Some forces want to keep the status quo and are threatened at the idea of change, even if it's a positive change. We've seen this over and over with false media attacks on groups working for change for poor people, for workers, and for the environment.

The situation has changed tremendously over the years with corporate control of media messages and more corporate ability to fund political candidates, more sophisticated attacks on change groups and leaders, and other kinds of issues we face, like budget deficits not only in our country, states, and communities but also in most of our organizations. With dire predictions of continued cuts in social justice funding, more environmental disasters, possible financial collapses, and more economic hardships coming our way, we must be prepared and plan for the long haul.

Preparing for these kinds of setbacks and attacks takes many different approaches. Many organizations and foundations are collaborating to protect groups with coordinated rapid response systems and simple tools to counter attacks. Unlike when I was first doing this work, some organizations are devoted to helping people understand how to both plan for problems and deal with them once they arise (see the resource list).

Having a long-term vision can both inspire us and keep us on track as we face many obstacles along the way. Collective visioning allows us to stay focused on the bigger picture despite the setbacks we experience. I'm not about to get disillusioned and give up, and I want to keep as many people working in their different ways alongside me and the many others I work with.

You can't really practice dealing with issues of crisis and setback. The response has to be developed in the moment. The important points are to get the group to revisit the vision, pay attention, ask questions, and develop a strategy to deal with the issues that the group is facing while staying connected to the vision.

Here are some guidelines for dealing with a crisis:

1. Try to *be prepared* as much as possible. Have a plan for what you will do if you were to be attacked by a media source or lost your biggest funding source. Practice together and role-play how you would handle these situations.

2. When a crisis arises, *bring your group together* immediately to talk about the issues, whether internal like a financial setback or external like an environmental crisis or a media attack. Do not try to hide or keep secrets from your group. This tactic almost always comes back to harm you and your group.

3. Before starting to address what's happening, remind people to *review the vision*, why they work for and love the organization, and what accomplishments the group has achieved. Review agreements. In a time of crisis, these are more important than at any other time. If you have a habit of opening with a song, a reading, or a moment of silence, do what you would normally do. This grounds people and keeps them from panic or blame.

4. *Lay out the full issue, problem, or situation* for the whole group, inviting others to speak from their side of the story.

5. *Start problem solving with the group.* Keep the vision and the goals in mind as you come up with new strategies. Once you have ideas for what the whole group wants to

do, you might consider breaking into small groups to address different parts of the plan, such as communication (internal/external), outreach, and fund-raising.

If the crisis is within the group, I strongly recommend using a third-party facilitator—someone experienced with group dynamics. It can make the difference in whether a group implodes or moves forward.

Here's a story that illustrates how a group can respond to attacks and setbacks using the above guidelines.

overcoming setbacks and attacks: the real story

In the late '80s, the Piedmont Peace Project held a successful press conference announcing that we planned to sue the state for illegally denying us access to register voters on public property. The next day the North Carolina state attorney released a false statement saying the state had not denied us this access and was considering a countersuit against the Piedmont Peace Project for filing what the state attorney called a frivolous lawsuit.

The Kannapolis newspaper published a vicious attack on PPP, even though it had proof of the true story: copies of letters we gave them from the state attorney denying our right to register voters. However, the paper refused to print a retraction or to write the truth.

Immediately, our members felt disempowered and were prepared to give up. Many even believed the newspaper reports and thought that they had somehow been duped. We held an emergency meeting and asked everyone to talk about how they were feeling. We then asked people to think of a time that the newspaper had made false statements. All of a sudden, the energy shifted as people began to pour out their stories. Some were personal stories of published accusations that were untrue, and others were stories about how the paper had printed articles claiming that "colored" people were less smart than others and didn't deserve the right to vote. People remembered stories in the paper about how black people had incited violence by wanting to integrate the schools and stories of fear and hatred around labor and civil rights organizing.

After the telling of many stories, including some that went back to the '40s and '50s, we brought people back to our vision of what we wanted and planned to do and discussed why we were a threat to those in power. People realized that we had been successful in unseating some local politicians who were known members of the KKK and that, for the first time, our community had elected people of color. Of course we were a threat to the people who had always held power in that community.

A holiday weekend was coming up, so we had to decide what our counterstrategy would be. We wrote our own press release, shrunk the two letters from the state to half size, and printed them on the back of the press release. Because our community had a large number of people who could not read, many churches had a tradition of reading aloud important news or letters that affected their congregations. So we made hundreds of copies to pass out to everyone and then went around the surrounding communities and found every express mail envelope we could get our hands on. On Saturday, we put in the envelopes a cover note to the ministers with the press release, asking them to stand for truth and justice and read our letter aloud to their congregations. We then slid the express envelopes under the front doors of every church in the area so that they would be found first thing Sunday morning and delivered to the minister. Many of our members knew the ministers or attended the churches. They made requests that the letter be read publicly and that people be encouraged to call the newspaper to print the real story. The next day, we continued to pass out the press releases to all the surrounding businesses, also asking the owners to call the newspaper office.

After two days, we received a call from the newspaper saying it would print our story. Our press release was printed almost word for word. The state announced that of course we could register people to vote in public places—it was the law—and we dropped the lawsuit and never heard anything else from the state about the countersuit. Our members got a valuable lesson in standing up for their rights and not letting an "official" source of news define their truth.

Although today we have many alternative ways to communicate our messages, many poor communities still do not have access to the new technology, although even that is quickly changing, as computers become more accessible and our children are growing up with them. However, I also believe that what we did in the late '80s was much more effective than if we'd had access to current technology because the actions we took involved the whole community.

Through organizing and bringing our members back to the original vision, we were able to turn this potential catastrophe around and win a powerful victory against the state, while forcing the newspaper to tell the real story.

What follows next is a story that illustrates all the actions I have mentioned in this chapter: cultural shifts about power and a positive focus, cultivation of visionary leadership, and strategies for facing setbacks.

working for the long haul: education, not incarceration

This is a story about a community that worked many years to close down a prison so awful that a *New York Times* article once said, "Here in the middle of the impoverished Mississippi Delta is a juvenile prison so rife with brutality, cronyism and neglect that many legal experts say it is the worst in the nation."[1] The small town of Tallulah, Louisiana, once a thriving community, is one of the poorest communities in the country, with one of the worst school systems as well, due to the effects of the privately owned prison in their community.

Although the community was successful in closing the youth prison, the facility was immediately turned into a prison for adults. Facing such a blow after so much hard work would have ended the efforts in many groups, but this community created a collective vision of what they wanted instead of a prison and accomplished goals that many thought were impossible along the way.

"When the prison came to town [November 1994] most people weren't even aware of what it was going to be," Hayward Fair, a local leader and veteran civil rights activist, said. "It was something that produced jobs and people needed jobs so there wasn't no real resistance to it." But the local economy was devastated, and Fair blamed the prison.

"It's killing the economy of the area, in my opinion," he said. "Prisons only bring money to the owners."[2]

The youth prison became infamous for terrible conditions and abuse. About six weeks after it opened its doors, a federal judge declared a state of emergency "due to riots and an inability of staff to control and protect youth."[3] In 1995, Human Rights Watch reported that the Tallulah facility violated international human rights. In 1996, the US Department of Justice wrote a letter to Governor Mike Foster informing him of "life-threatening and dangerous" conditions at the state's juvenile facility. In 1998 the US Justice Department filed suit accusing the State of Louisiana of failing to protect youthful inmates from brutality by guards and providing inadequate education, medical care, and mental health care.[4]

Mothers of incarcerated children with organizations such as Families and Friends of Louisiana's Incarcerated Children (FFLIC) and the Juvenile Justice Project of Louisiana (JJPL) began to work to try to close the prison. At first, the mothers of incarcerated children and the community of Tallulah were in conflict. In an interview with Xochitl Bervera, an organizer who worked on the project, she said, "The community fought the closure of the prison because they were unbelievably poor and it was the largest employer in the parish! Many people in the town hated FFLIC and JJPL for giving them a bad name—the campaign, after all, was called Close Tallulah Now! and Tallulah was their town! The mothers felt that everyone in that town was a collaborator in their sons' abuse and neglect. One leader of FFLIC said she refused to buy gas, cigarettes, or even a soft drink in the town and would wait till she crossed the town line."

When I spoke with community leader Moses Williams in the summer of 2010, he said one reason that the local public school system was so bad was that the Tallulah Correctional Facility for Youth (one of the several names it was called during the time it was open) was required to have a school system with certified teachers. The state paid better than the local public schools could afford to, so the town's schools lost many certified teachers. After the facility opened the Westside School for the juvenile inmates, less than 40 percent of the teachers in Tallulah public schools were certified to teach. This was devastating for the youth of the town, and the effects are still being felt today. Williams said he was deeply affected about the ramifications of these actions when he heard Cecil Picard, secretary of education for Louisiana, say, in Williams's words "that a student that has an uncertified teacher for three consecutive years cannot recover from the effect—that child is lost as far as education," and Williams believes this has proved to be true in Tallulah.

After about ten years of organizing efforts, FFLIC and JJPL finally won passage of a bill signed into law by the state legislature in 2003 to close down the facility prison as a youth prison by spring 2004. Once the community realized that the prison was going to close to juveniles, Xochitl said, "The question of 'what next?' was on the table." An amazing thing happened. The mothers and the community came together and formed a coalition of organizations called Northeast Louisiana Delta Coalition for Education and Economic Development to work together to come up with a vision to answer that question.

As the mothers of incarcerated children prepared to celebrate the closing of the youth prison, they were hit with another setback. The state legislature announced that the facility would be reopening as an adult prison. The town became split between those who did not want a prison to be the thing that defined their community or the only thing their children saw on their way to school and those who saw the prison as a place that provided critically needed jobs and income.

This is part of a recurring theme for those of us working for social justice. Every time we win a victory, another obstacle is thrown in our path. Without an alternative vision of what we want for our communities, we will just keep fighting for small victories, so difficult to achieve and so difficult to hold on to, always in a defensive posture. We're holding our finger in the dike to keep the floods from crashing down on us.

But the mothers, now joined with the community, did not give up. Under the leadership of Hayward Fair, Moses Williams, and others, they created a collective vision of what they wanted for their community instead of a prison. Local leaders and citizens in the coalition went to work. After knocking on about fifteen hundred doors and talking to everyone they could, they decided that they needed a learning center and community college instead of a prison. They began to remind folks that the prison had failed to bring the economic boom it had promised at the outset. Many people agreed that it would be wonderful if kids could pass by a community learning center instead of a prison on their way to high school.

Jane Wholey, who was a member of the coalition— which included community leaders and organizers from FFLIC, JJPL, Grassroots Leadership, and Building Blocks for Youth, among others—came in from New Orleans to help the group develop a media campaign to celebrate the closing of the youth prison and to highlight the members' vision for their community. I heard the story of what happened on the day the prison was scheduled to close in spring 2004 from several people I interviewed. On that day, community members gathered to tell the world their dreams. The tall fence gate, beneath the sign of the prison and topped with shiny silver razor wire, was the backdrop for their national press conference.

Leaders and mothers spoke about their victory in closing down the youth prison and named their concerns about its continued presence as a prison for adults. The community and the mothers were so strong in the ways that they came together and prayed together. Two state senators who had opposed each other—Senator Charles Jones, who represented the parish and had fought the closure, and Senator Don Cravins, who had authored the closure bill, appeared together in unity. Then a young woman who was a student came to the podium. She said, "We want to present to you our vision for our community instead of this prison."

All of a sudden, music filled the air—"Pomp and Circumstance." From behind the house across the street, high school students came marching, all dressed in caps and gowns. Each girl carried a single rose. The students lined up in front of the prison gates and released a banner. It read, "Tallulah Community College, Class of 2006." The young woman then asked their state senator to come up and give a mock commencement speech to the class of 2006. Senator Jones came to the stage and in a very emotional, impassioned speech he promised the community that he would

put forth a bill to turn this thirty-three-building prison into
an educational center housing a community college, con-
solidated high school, and community center.

During the next few months, the organizers worked
with community members, including children, to develop
a vision of what the learning center and community college
of their dreams would look like. I helped lead a visioning
process as part of that work. We worked with "flyover" pictures of the prison that were developed from a computer
model since we were not allowed in and didn't have blue-
prints of the layout.

In the visioning with the children and other community
members, I asked them to describe what they thought a college was. Then I asked them to identify what they felt their
community needed. The two lists were totally inconsis-
tent, so we ripped up the sheet on which we had described
a college and redesigned what a college should be to meet
the needs of the community. Their college had an adult
learning center and an auto mechanic school. It offered
training in health care services, business, and art. It even
had restaurants—a McDonald's and a French restaurant.
When I asked the young boy who had suggested the French
restaurant if he liked French food, he replied, "I don't know,
but I hear it's very good."

After the visioning sessions, young artists and architects
came in to help the community create a viable model of their
vision of a community learning center and college. Some of
the children's ideas for the community college included a
sports complex, a day-care center, and even an attached area
or corridor for students to run businesses needed by the
community. It also had a center for elder care, since many

people could not go to college because they needed to care for family members.

On June 5, 2005, the community held another press conference to show the community college of their dreams. The children had created large art pieces depicting their visions of themselves in the future. They drew doctors, lawyers, teachers, police officers, psychologists, and even a nail manicurist. The art formed a walk-in twenty-by-twenty-foot structure that stood ten feet tall.

Working from this vision, the community continued to organize, working with allies, lawyers, and elected representatives to win the first victory of its kind in the United States—the Louisiana legislature voted to turn the prison into a community college and learning center.

In my interview in August 2010 with Xochitl Bervera, who was working in 2004–2005 as a staff member for Families and Friends of Louisiana's Incarcerated Children and Grassroots Leadership and deeply involved in the organizing with local community members, she said, "This was an incredible victory. It was the first time in the United States that a law was passed to turn a prison into a learning center and community college."

On July 11, 2005, Governor Kathleen Blanco signed Act 721, creating the Northeast Delta Learning Center. Most legislative pundits had believed that the learning center bill would die in committee. "Nobody gave us a chance of winning," said Hayward Fair. "But that's been our history."[5]

I wish I could end this story with "and they all lived happily ever after." While the community prepared for the next phase of their winning campaign—to present a budget request to secure the funds to turn their victory into a reality—Katrina hit.

As the community opened its arms to refugees escaping the floodwaters in New Orleans, they watched their dreams of a community college get washed away with the disaster facing the state. Not only were the funds unavailable to follow through on this historic promise, but the prison became a temporary refuge for incarcerated flood victims from New Orleans.

So why do I tell a story that has an unfinished ending? It's important to see and remember the amazing victory that was accomplished once the community turned to a vision of what they wanted instead of what they were against. Tallulah is one tiny low-income community in a state that has faced devastation. The people may not have achieved their dream—yet—but in the meantime, they stand as hope for all of us, an example of what is possible when we work from a place of vision, a place of hope.

The community continues to work for the learning center today. In my interview with Moses Williams, he said, "It is still our hope and vision that one day our state will create a regional institution in the delta parishes that will truly focus on higher education and workforce development and focus less on the development of private prisons as a tool for economic development."

In an interview in 2007, a reporter with *Left Turn* magazine asked Hayward Fair, who is now in his seventies, what kept him in the struggle. "I ain't struggling, I'm free," he answered. He explained that this struggle is not about him. "I see the young people in the community that need help.

That's what keeps me going. If you see something and you feel it aint [sic] right, don't say they ought to change it, get in there, roll your sleeves up and say let's change it. That's the only way. You gotta keep a cool head and do the thing that's right. When you know right and fight for it, you're gonna win."[6]

All I have to say to that is "Yes!"

chapter takeaways

In this chapter, we looked at how to sustain strong groups that help us reach our collective visions. Here are some points to take away:

- Cultural shifts in how we think about power help us support—and be—strong leaders.
- Collective visioning supports a cultural shift to focus on work that is positive and affirming.
- We need to cultivate visionary and shared leadership.
- A plan grounded in a collective vision helps a group get through setbacks and attacks.
- When dealing with a crisis, it helps to be prepared, come together, review the vision, lay out the issue, and start problem solving.

exercise 8

The goal of this exercise is to show that a group doesn't have to have only one leader; we all have leadership qualities, and together we can provide the leadership we need or identify what's missing that we need to bring in.

Shared Leadership

This is a leadership assessment exercise that I do with community folks, especially when they don't think of themselves as leaders.

Start by asking people to identify what makes a good leader—the qualities or skills that are needed. The group will most likely create a long list, with items like these:

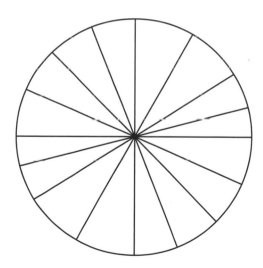

Figure 6 **Leadership Wheel**

good speaker, visionary, problem solver, organizer, writer, manager, good fund-raiser, respected member of the community, and so on.

Next, ask people who among them has all of these qualities. So far, in my experience, no one has ever raised a hand to say that he or she has all of them.

Then, draw a circle like a wheel with as many spokes on it as there are items on the list.

Ask each person in the room to name one quality from the leadership list that he or she has. Write the leadership quality on one spoke of the wheel and add the person's name to the wedge of space. If other people have the same quality, add their names to the space as well.

If some people don't know what they might be good at or are shy about saying so, get their friends to help. Sometimes people will add things like making phone calls for outreach or organizing the potlucks. One time, a woman agreed only that she was good at cleaning the office. We put that down but encouraged her to come to all our workshops. She eventually became the leader for getting out the vote in her community.

After everyone's name is on the chart, ask about other qualities on the list that don't yet appear on the wheel. Some people are good at several things, and the group can decide where they are needed most. In some cases, the list may include a quality that the group doesn't possess. For example, when the folks at the Piedmont Peace Project did this exercise, we realized that we needed someone who could do an economic analysis. We recruited a Harvard student from Boston to help us in that area. Groups have gone outside of their organizations to recruit people with special skills they need and don't have, such as photographers, media experts, architects, and so on. Or a group might decide to get one or more of their members trained in an important skill that they don't yet have.

Next, ask how many of the people whose names are on the chart can actually commit time. Then, ask someone who is good at a certain activity—for example, fundraising or speaking—if he or she would teach one or two volunteers how to do that activity, and ask for volunteers who would like to learn these skills.

The Next Step: Hope, Vision, and Action

To be hopeful in bad times is not just foolishly
romantic.... What we choose to emphasize in
this complex history will determine our lives....
And if we do act, in however small a way,
we don't have to wait for some grand
utopian future.

HOWARD ZINN

In writing this book, I've focused very little on
"what's wrong" in our country and the world. We
get enough of that every time we turn on the news or open
a newspaper or go online to see what's happening. I wanted
to give you a different message, a message of hope. But we
also have to look at the reality around us.

Every day we are flooded with bad news: the economy
and unemployment are getting worse; human-made disasters are destroying our environment; homelessness, hunger,
disease, and the hatred of others are all rising; our education system is suffering; and violence in increasing. Every
day, we hear more information about how big corporations,

the mainstream media, and a few rich people are control-
ling our lives, our society, and our government. We live in
the richest country in the world, but despite our economy
being mired in the deepest recession since the 1930s, people
in the top 1 percent continue to own as much wealth as
those in the bottom 90 percent.[1] Another way to look at it
is the top 10 percent of people in this country owns 85 percent of the wealth, while 90 percent of us own 15 percent
of the wealth.[2]

What's probably the most disturbing for me is what our
young people are thinking. Most of them do not hold a
positive vision for the future. If asked, they say that their
lives will be worse in the future. If we continue on the path
we're on now, that will become a reality.

Earlier in the book, I wrote about how I sometimes ask
folks I'm leading in visioning to bring in a picture of a child
or young person in their lives, someone they can picture
living the future that we're working to create. I'd like to tell
you about a young person in my life named James. James
was hit by a bomb in Afghanistan while I was working on
this book.

I recently returned from spending a week at the hospital
by his bedside. When I first saw him there, he had metal
pins that stuck out all over his left leg like some kind of
giant Erector set. His leg was attached to a rope holding
it high up toward the ceiling. I burst out crying. At one
point, a staff person asked me not to cry in front of him,
and everyone who knew us laughed, saying that if I quit
crying, James would think he was dying or something. He's
had thirteen surgeries, with several more to go, and has a

rough road ahead of him, but he's very much alive. The doctors are predicting a recovery time of two to three years, but they're not sure how much use of his leg he will have. Amputation is still a consideration.

While I was at the hospital, young men and women were brought in on a daily basis—many much worse off than James. Some of the wounded were too young to even shave. We learned that students are allowed to prejoin the military in high school at sixteen and seventeen and get "pretraining" at base camp after their junior year and return for their senior year. At the age of eighteen, they're ready to be deployed. Most of the kids we talked with were between eighteen and twenty. Almost every one we talked to joined because of poverty, the promise of specialized training, the need to support his or her family, or the promise of an education. In James's case, he was promised he would be trained in computers, never go to war, and have his college loans paid off, only to be told as soon as he joined that the college loan program no longer existed and he would be trained as a truck driver.

So right now, I'm thinking about James and about all of the other young people I saw at the hospital who felt forced to join the military as their way out of poverty. I'm thinking about all of the newly disabled people in Iraq and Afghanistan. I'm picturing James putting on T-shirts and boxers sewn with Velcro so that he can dress himself again, and I'm thinking of what the next step will be so that James and all of these other young people can have a future that we all want for them—and for ourselves. Finishing this book is, for me, another step.

So how do we hold hope in the face of terrible things? Sitting quietly by and not doing anything is to make a choice to let matters continue to get worse.

We can change the situation. We can turn it around. This is a country built on freedom and equality (although not for everyone), but we have to take back our government and create a true democracy that we control. We have to create a world that works for everyone. We do that by taking the first step, then the next, and then joining with others taking those steps, walking together to build a powerful movement for change.

It starts first with a shift in our own consciousness. It starts when we hold a vision of justice for all. It starts when we begin to make the cultural shifts needed to create a positive, powerful movement that can change our lives at every level.

To make this cultural shift, we need to do four things:

• Move from obsessively focusing on the individual to thinking about the collective.
• Work together to build trust and community across our many differences.
• Create a collective positive vision of the future we want.
• Reach out to allies, friends, family, and our broader community, not just to people who believe what we do, but to all who value a just and sustainable world.

And then, we have to take all of this to the next step: *action!* As a Japanese proverb says, "Vision without action is a daydream, but action without vision is a nightmare."

If you are part of a group working for change, how do you help your group become more effective, work from a positive vision, and connect with other groups that share your vision? If you are not already part of an organization working to make changes, how do you find a group to take action with?

Reading this book is only a first step, an individual step. If you don't have a group, organize one. It could be made up of family members, a church group, neighbors, or friends you have coffee with around the kitchen table once a week. Invite a diverse group of people to come together to begin to build community and to vision for the future you want.

You could start a book club, beginning with this book. Discuss each chapter and the exercises at the end, and then decide on a first action step. Or go to the Q&A page on my website for information about groups in your area and how you can get more involved. You can also find out how to get trained as a facilitator to lead collective visioning or to build powerful and diverse networks.

Take a first step toward action. Only you know what that should be.

Remember, it's not a mistake if you try something and it doesn't work; it's a learning process. The only mistake is to give up. I have done many things in my work for change over the past thirty years that I wish I could do over, and I have hurt some people along the way. But you can only keep moving forward, doing the best you can. Always evaluate and see what worked and look at what you would do differently next time. Talk to people. Keep asking and listening. Ask what would make someone want to come to a gathering, potluck, or dinner (don't use the word "meeting"!) to talk about what our hopes are for the future and what we can do together to get there.

We have to change the way we work for change. I often use a common phrase we've all heard: "mind, body, and soul."

What are the mind, body, and soul of creating a movement for positive change?

The *mind* is critical in providing us with the research, analysis, and grounding of information that support all the other work we do for change—it's what supports the body of our work. It's the expert knowledge we gather, but more importantly, it's the innate knowledge we have within us. Many organizations provide the information that supports our work, but you also have to trust what you know is right for you and your community.

The *body* is the action we take—the people-to-people, door-to-door work that has to be done in our communities and organizations to make change happen. We can't do the work without the mind, but the mind is useless without the body.

The *soul* of creating a movement for change is the heart, and it is the part that is most often left out of our work. The soul or heart of our work is about who or what inspires and leads us. It is about connection—our relationships with each other and how we work together. It is about how we link our different issues and build networks and coalitions so we equal *more than the sum of our parts.*

We have the information. We have the numbers. And we have the ability to change the world. But we need to work across the boundaries of race, class, identities, issues, and strategies.

We need to embody a different way of working that can truly win—a way that can transform the world. In order to do this we have to learn how to include the soul of movement building in our work. We must work from a place of vision, a place of hope, a place of joy, and a place that is grounded in our hearts.

To build a winning movement that mobilizes millions of people, we can't continue to focus on only what's wrong. We must offer a vision of what's possible.

We must build a movement that reflects our values; a movement that nurtures and supports us as activists, as individuals, *and* as families; a movement that feeds our hearts and our souls.

notes

Preface

1. Lawrence Wittner, "What Activists Can Learn from the Nuclear Freeze Movement," History News Network, August 18, 2003, http://www.us/articles/1636.html.
2. Ibid.
3. Ibid.
4. Developed by Dr. Kathleen Sullivan for the International Campaign to Abolish Nukes.

Chapter 1

1. For more information, see http://www.yayainc.com.
2. Stacy A. Teicher, "New Year, New School Concepts in New Orleans," *Christian Science Monitor*, August 24, 2006, http.//www.csmonitor.com/2006/0824/p15s01-legn.html.

Chapter 2

1. *Interview with Vincent and Rosemarie Harding*, Veterans of Hope Pamphlet Series 1, no. 5 (Denver: The Veterans of Hope Project, February 2001).
2. Howard Gardner authored the theory of multiple intelligences. Go to http://www.pz.harvard.edu to learn more about Project Zero, where he was codirector for twenty-five years, working with colleagues to apply this theory.
3. Christina Baldwin, *Storycatcher: Making Sense of Our Lives through the Power and Practice of Story* (Novato, CA: New World Library, 2007).

Chapter 3

1. Mathew Davis, "Critical Pedagogy and Social Justice in the 21st Century: From a High School Student's Perspective" (speech, Alternative Education Resource Organization conference, Albany, NY, June 26, 2009), www.educationrevolution .org/2009freevideos.html.
2. Barbara Ehrenreich, *Bright-Sided: How Positive Thinking Is Undermining America* (New York: Picador Publishers, 2010).
3. Rhonda Byrne, *The Secret* (New York: Atria Books, 2006).
4. Rhonda Byrne, *The Power* (New York: Atria Books, 2010).

Chapter 4

1. Constitution Society, http://www.constitution.org/col/blind _men.htm.

Chapter 5

1. Starhawk, *Webs of Power: Notes from the Global Uprising* (Gabriola Island, BC: New Society Publishers, 2002).
2. Joanna Macy and Molly Young Brown, *Coming Back to Life: Practices to Reconnect Our Lives, Our World* (Gabriola Island, BC: New Society Publishers, 1998).
3. As rated by Council for a Livable World voting records.
4. As rated by AFL-CIO voting records.
5. Macy and Brown, *Coming Back to Life*.
6. Caroline Framke, "Ann Curry's NBC 'Dateline' Special Puts Spotlight on America's Poorest," Women's Media Center, July 22, 2010, http://womensmediacenter.com/blog/2010/07 /ann-currys-dateline-special-puts-spotlight-on-americas-poor/.

Chapter 6

1. Carol J. Castaneda, "Protesters No Longer Seen as Radicals," *USA Today*, January 14, 1991.
2. I told the story about the community's vision to be annexed and receive services from the surrounding city in my first book, *Bridging the Class Divide*.

3. Shaila Dewan, "In County Made Rich by Golf, Some Enclaves Are Left Behind," *New York Times*, June 7, 2005.
4. Hannah Sharpe, "Habitat, Midway Celebrate Start of New Housing," *Southern Pines (NC) Pilot*, Wednesday, June 9, 2010.

Chapter 7
1. Fox Butterfield, "Hard Time: A Special Report; Profits at a Juvenile Prison Come with a Chilling Cost," *New York Times*, July 15, 1998.
2. Jordan Flaherty, "Education versus Incarceration in Tallulah, Louisiana," *Left Turn*, November 14 , 2007, http://www.leftturn .org/education-versus-incarceration-tallulah-louisiana.
3. Xochitl Berrera, "The Death of Tallulah Prison," *ColorLines*, June 24, 2004.
4. Fox Butterfield, "U.S. Suing Louisiana On Prison Ills," *New York Times*, November 6, 1998.
5. Flaherty, "Education versus Incarceration."
6. Ibid.

Conclusion
1. "The Growing Divide," United for Fair Economy, http://www .faireconomy.org/issues/growing_divide.
2. G. William Domhoff, "Power in America: Wealth, Income, and Power," WhoRulesAmerica.net, September 2005 (updated September 2010), http://sociology.ucsc.edu/whorulesamerica /power/wealth.html.

Acknowledgments
1. For more information, see www.listeningproject.info.
2. For more information, see http://www.positivechange.org/.
3. Diana Whitney, David Cooperrider, Amanda Trosten-Bloom, and Brian S. Kaplin, *Encyclopedia of Positive Questions*, vol. 1, *Using Appreciative Inquiry to Bring Out the Best in Your Organization*, (Cleveland: Crown Custom Publishing, 2001).
4. Fran Peavey, *Strategic Questioning: An Approach to Creating Personal and Social Change*, ed. Vivian Hutchinson (updated 1997).

resources

Books

Backstein, Karen. *The Blind Men and the Elephant* (New York: Cartwheel Books, 1992).

Baldwin, Christina. *Storycatcher: Making Sense of Our Lives through the Power and Practice of Story* (Novato, CA: New World Library, 2007).

Baldwin, Christina, and Anne Linnea. *The Circle Way: A Leader in Every Chair* (San Francisco: Berrett-Koehler Publishers, 2010).

Cooperrider, David, and Diana Whitney. *Appreciative Inquiry: A Positive Revolution in Change* (San Francisco: Berrett-Koehler Publishers, 2005).

Lakey, George. *Facilitating Group Learning: Strategies for Success with Adult Learners* (San Francisco: Jossey-Bass, 2010).

Starhawk. *Truth or Dare: Encounters with Power, Authority, and Mystery* (San Francisco: Harper, 1988).

Whitney, Diana, Amanda Trosten-Bloom, and Kae Rader. *Appreciative Leadership: Focus on What Works to Drive Winning Performance and Build a Thriving Organization* (New York: McGraw-Hill, 2010).

Tools

The Praxis Project's simplified adaption of the SCOPE Power Analysis: http://www.thepraxisproject.org/irc/organizing.html.

The Strategic Concepts in Organizing and Policy Education (SCOPE) *Power Tools Manual*, which covers advanced power analysis and more: http://www.scopela.org/section.php?id=66.

Training

POWER UP Networks: http://www.powerupnetworks.org.

Training for Change: http://www.trainingforchange.org.

Appreciative Inquiry: http://www.positivechange.org/appreciative
-inquiry-consultants/diana-whitney.html.

For a more extensive list of resources, go to http://www.lindastout
.org.

acknowledgments

First, I have to begin with family because without them I could have done none of this. To Angela Barth, my best friend and soulmate, who has supported me throughout this process by taking care of all my needs from cleaning to laundry, making sure I ate, and supporting and always believing in me when I doubted I could do this. To my sister, Renae, who volunteered to help type up handwritten stories, organize my office, and do other administrative tasks, and to my friend and coworker Connie Fitzgerald, who manages Spirit in Action and who supported my writing process and my health and took up the slack during my absence from work.

As I mentioned earlier, I often use "we" or "us" instead of "I" or "me" in this book. That is because so many people added to the formation of these ideas, and without all of these contributions, Spirit in Action would not have been able to produce the methodology we use successfully today. Many of the ideas come from knowledge that has been with us for ages from our indigenous ancestors.

Much of our methodology came from Spirit in Action's first experimental grassroots Circles of Change. These took place all over the country, with twenty-seven trained facilitators and the hundreds of people who participated and shared their knowledge and learnings with us. We have had a strong team of staff, volunteers, and consultants who have come together to help create the work we do today.

Among those many folks I want to honor are Carolyn Cushing, who has worked with Spirit in Action from the beginning and is now director of the Progressive Communicators Network; the first visioning team that helped form the Circles of Change, Jerry Koch-Gonzales, Starhawk, Fran Peavey, George Lakey, Leah Wise, Jane Sapp, and John Lapham, and the late Bill Moyer and Felice Yeskel, whom we love and miss; and all of those who were part of the visioning of developing Spirit in Action. To our consultants who have helped us on this journey: Sharon Vardatira, Sharon Coney, Phyllis Labanowski, Pamela Freeman, Jane Wholey, Connie Fitzgerald, Betty Burkes, Jane Midgley, Diane Johnson, Guadalupe Guajardo, Andrew Gaines, Rose Sackey Milligan, Roberto Vargas, Susan Bergeron-West, and Kathleen Sharkey.

And to all those who were facilitators of some of the first experimental Circles of Change: Laura Loecher, Catherine Hoffman, Bethsaida Ruiz, Karen Hutchinson, Arrington Chambliss, Skylar Fein, Natalie Reteneller, Toni Lester, Richard Ford, Phyllis Robinson, Carlos Turriago, Lydia Cabasco, Nijmie Dzurinko, Jose Lopez, Maura Wolf, Patricia Rojas Zambrano, Darnell Johnson, Megan Voorhees, Scherazade King, Susan Leslie, Paula Cole Jones, Audra Friend, Bill Aal, and Margo Adair (in loving memory of Margo, who passed on September 2, 2010).

And a very special thanks to our current trainers and facilitators who work for us, Gopal Dayaneni, Jodi Lasseter,

Taij Kumarie Moteelall, and Manauvaskar Kublall, and our board members Tom Louie, Neal Adams, and Ferdene Chin-Yee.

I want to thank all of the Spirit in Action Circle of Change facilitators and participants who led and were part of groups throughout the country. I know I've left out many people's names; I apologize and thank you for your contributions.

In addition, I want to appreciate all of our supporters and donors who have made our transformational work possible. For many it was a stretch, a risk, to fund a new way of working, and for others it had been something they had always looked for. From my longest donor and supporter of thirty years, my dear friend Robbie Kunreuther; to all of our donors, some who have supported me for twenty-five-plus years throughout my social change work life—from the Piedmont Peace Project till now (you know who you are!); to Laura Loecher, who made the first donation when Spirit in Action was just a dream; and to all of our founding donors to those who have just started supporting our work, know that without your alliance and support, the work could not happen.

And now to all those who helped me in the writing process. Thanks to my writing coach, Mary Beth Averill, who gave me support and writing exercises to help me when I got stuck and helped me learn how to write a proposal. And a very special thanks to Susan Stinson, my friend and an amazing author who inspires me and who supported me by reading, editing, encouraging, and keeping me laughing throughout the process. She is fabulous, skillful, sensitive, patient, and funny. Here's to working together on many more projects!

I would also like to thank my agent, Rita Rosenkrantz, who believed in my project from the beginning. To Johanna Vondeling at Berrett-Koehler, who said, "I love your proposal, but I think it's about five or six books," and hung in and supported me to write a new proposal for this book. And of course, to all the staff at Berrett-Koehler, especially my editor, Neal Maillet, and the senior editor, Jeevan Sivasubramaniam. I also want to thank the amazing final editor of this process, Sharon Goldinger.

I want to thank those I have learned from and been inspired by: Herb Walters with Listening Project[1] who taught me about asking questions for social change; Appreciative Inquiry,[2] for teaching me about framing and asking questions (see *Encyclopedia of Positive Questions*[3]); and Fran Peavey's work on strategic questioning.[4]

I want to appreciate the work of Sara Knight and Jen Angel with Aid and Abet, who helped with media and the book tour; Gail and Betsy Leondar-Wright, for radio promotion; and Tim Grahl and staff, who created my website. Without them, you might not know about this book.

In addition to all of our collective knowledge, it's important to remember that we all stand on the knowledge of many others who have passed their wisdom down to us. I want to honor my mentors—my parents, Kathleen and Herschel Stout; Septima Clark; Ron Charity; Studs Terkel; Howard Zinn; and Elise Boulding—who have all passed on. Also, all those who have mentored me in my work as an organizer who still work for justice: Cathy Howell, Si Kahn, John Wancheck, Laura Chasin, Ron Miller, Michael Lerner, Joanna Macy, and Starhawk.

As I have learned from my elders and peers, I have also come to learn from the younger activists in my life: from junior high school students in New Orleans to the young leaders that I have the privilege of working with; the folks at Young People's Project, Tracy Van Slyke, Isaac Graves, Joel Lehi Organista, and Joshua Wolfsun; and my niece and nephews, Byron Parker and Tony, Adam, and Amy Barth, as well as the young Spirit in Action staff and too many others to name. They inspire me, challenge my thinking, and make me want to work for a better world for them to inherit.

index

about Spirit in Action

SPIRIT IN ACTION supports a transformational culture shift in organizing—a culture of positive vision, connection across traditional barriers, and diversity of voice, all united in heart and spirit. By listening deeply to social justice activists, Spirit in Action has developed a research-based methodology that integrates decades of hands-on experience in inclusive, broad-based movement building.

Spirit in Action's three core programs are grounded in the day-to-day reality of grassroots communities. Its distinctive facilitation process moves beyond just bringing people together; it builds the trust necessary to heal from divisions and act from the recognition of people's wholeness, interconnectedness, and interdependence.

• POWER UP Networks teaches people to create and advance networks for large-scale change. Networks are a powerful means to increase the capacity and impact of social change organizations. They ground people in a larger vision and create channels that enable that vision to spread. Thoughtfully built, networks harness and expand the energy of groups working toward the same goal, allowing them to be more than the sum of their parts. POWER UP Networks provides the support networks need to successfully leverage the strength of diverse strategies. This program guides individuals and groups to see themselves clearly and then to see beyond themselves to the larger progressive movement we share.

- Community Visioning and Organizing guides participants to work together more effectively, allowing a vast yet deeply aligned collective vision of the future to be cocreated. An atmosphere of openness allows respectful dialogue about controversial issues.

- Leadership Training draws on theory, experiential practice, and storytelling to equip community leaders with the tools they need for sustainable, effective social action.

about the author

LINDA STOUT grew up poor in North Carolina. Her father was a tenant farmer, later a factory worker, and her mother worked in the textile mills until she became disabled when Linda was five. Growing up in poverty, Linda wanted to make her community better but thought the only way to do that was through prayer and making small changes.

Organizers seemed to speak only to college-educated people who were also well-versed in politics and used a language that excluded her. But she began to realize that many others were like her: people who joined groups to work on issues that concerned them but dropped out because they didn't feel at home with those who spoke a theoretical language of change that felt disconnected from their experience. She decided that although she might not be able to be an organizer with the peace and women's movements, she could organize other poor people like herself.

Linda went on to become a community organizer with a keen awareness about the need to speak the language of people who didn't know the language of social change and organizing. Her awareness of her own roots and of the people she wanted to reach let her build the Piedmont Peace Project. One of the most successful grassroots organizations in the Southeast in the 1980s, PPP was formed in the midst of a daunting mix of well-organized corporate interests, including textile giant Cannon Mills, and icons of intolerance such as Senator Jesse Helms and the Ku Klux Klan. PPP made historic political and social change in local communities and brought Linda experiences such as writing her first book, *Bridging the Class Divide and Other Lessons for Grassroots Organizers*; being featured in the PBS documentary "The Rage for Democracy"; and appearing on a panel with Hillary Clinton and Bill Moyers on national public television.

Now, with Spirit in Action, the organization she founded in 2000, Linda follows her passion to make movements for change welcoming people of all backgrounds, not just college-educated, middle-class white people. She helps bring people together to build trust so that all voices are heard as part of creating a collective vision for the future. She loves her two dogs, Sassafras and Smidgen, and raises backyard pet chickens, some of which lay colored eggs.

Berrett–Koehler
Publishers

Berrett-Koehler is an independent publisher dedicated to an ambitious mission: *Creating a World That Works for All*.

We believe that to truly create a better world, action is needed at all levels—individual, organizational, and societal. At the individual level, our publications help people align their lives with their values and with their aspirations for a better world. At the organizational level, our publications promote progressive leadership and management practices, socially responsible approaches to business, and humane and effective organizations. At the societal level, our publications advance social and economic justice, shared prosperity, sustainability, and new solutions to national and global issues.

A major theme of our publications is "Opening Up New Space." Berrett-Koehler titles challenge conventional thinking, introduce new ideas, and foster positive change. Their common quest is changing the underlying beliefs, mindsets, institutions, and structures that keep generating the same cycles of problems, no matter who our leaders are or what improvement programs we adopt.

We strive to practice what we preach—to operate our publishing company in line with the ideas in our books. At the core of our approach is stewardship, which we define as a deep sense of responsibility to administer the company for the benefit of all of our "stakeholder" groups: authors, customers, employees, investors, service providers, and the communities and environment around us.

We are grateful to the thousands of readers, authors, and other friends of the company who consider themselves to be part of the "BK Community." We hope that you, too, will join us in our mission.

A BK Currents Book

This book is part of our BK Currents series. BK Currents books advance social and economic justice by exploring the critical intersections between business and society. Offering a unique combination of thoughtful analysis and progressive alternatives, BK Currents books promote positive change at the national and global levels. To find out more, visit **www.bkconnection.com**.

Berrett–Koehler
Publishers

A community dedicated to creating
a world that works for all

Visit Our Website: www.bkconnection.com

Read book excerpts, see author videos and Internet movies, read
our authors' blogs, join discussion groups, download book apps, find
out about the BK Affiliate Network, browse subject-area libraries of
books, get special discounts, and more!

Subscribe to Our Free E-Newsletter, the *BK Communiqué*

Be the first to hear about new publications, special discount offers,
exclusive articles, news about bestsellers, and more! Get on the list
for our free e-newsletter by going to **www.bkconnection.com**.

Get Quantity Discounts

Berrett-Koehler books are available at quantity discounts for orders
of ten or more copies. Please call us toll-free at (800) 929-2929 or
email us at **bkp.orders@aidcvt.com**.

Join the BK Community

BKcommunity.com is a virtual meeting place where people from
around the world can engage with kindred spirits to create a world
that works for all. **BKcommunity.com** members may create their own
profiles, blog, start and participate in forums and discussion groups,
post photos and videos, answer surveys, announce and register for
upcoming events, and chat with others online in real time. Please join
the conversation!